The Automated Lighting Programmer's Handbook

THE AUTOMATED LIGHTING PROGRAMMER'S HANDBOOK

BRAD SCHILLER

AMSTERDAM • BOSTON • HEIDELBERG • LONDON
NEW YORK • OXFORD • PARIS • SAN DIEGO
SAN FRANCISCO • SINGAPORE • SYDNEY • TOKYO

Focal Press is an imprint of Elsevier

ISBN-13: 978- 0-240-80602-0
ISBN-10: 0-240-80602-6

British Library Cataloguing-in-Publication Data
A catalogue record for this book is available from the British Library.

The publisher offers special discounts on bulk orders of this book.
For information, please contact:

Manager of Special Sales
Elsevier
200 Wheeler Road
Burlington, MA 01803
Tel: 781-313-4700
Fax: 781-313-4882

For information on all Focal Press publications available, contact our World Wide Web home page at: http://www.focalpress.com

10 9 8 7 6 5 4 3 2

Printed in the United States of America

I would like to dedicate this book first to my grandfather, Maurice, who always encouraged everyone in the family to write. Then to my parents, Don and Annette, for teaching me "the best job is one you love." Finally, I dedicate this book to my wife, Margaret, and son, Matthew, for their continued support of my career.

Contents

List of Tables and Figures

Acknowledgements

I strongly believe in sharing my knowledge of automated lighting with others. I could not have gained my knowledge and experience without the assistance of many great people and organizations.

First I would like to thank High End Systems and Flying Pig Systems for the great exposure to the industry. During my six and a half years working as an employee of High End Systems, I was able to learn much more than I could have ever expected. There are too many names to list, but I thank everyone involved with both organizations throughout the years.

Next I would like to thank Pro Lights and Staging News (PLSN) for inspiring me to write on the subject of automated lighting programming. My monthly column "Feeding the Machines" was the catalyst for this book. Terry Lowe, Richard Cadena, and Bruce Jorhdal have all been very enthusiastic when encouraging my writing.

In addition, I would like to thank all the professional programmers and designers that I have met throughout the years. Our industry is a great one with many creative and intelligent people. We all contribute our skills and knowledge to continually improve our fast changing business. I especially would like to express thanks to the many that were able to participate in this book by providing a quote for Chapter 11.

Finally, I would like to thank you for reading this book and having an interest in programming automated lights. Whether programming is a hobby or a career choice, I am sure you will find it a fulfilling, challenging, fun, and expressive skill that you will enjoy every time you sit down behind a lighting console.

Introduction

I find working as an Automated Lighting Programmer a truly wonderful career choice. It enables me to travel throughout the world, meet many different people, and work on all types of productions. Each event presents a different set of challenges and opportunities. I always enjoy sharing my knowledge in this field with others and hope to do just that with this book.

Automated lighting is a fairly new development in our industry and there are many that are only now beginning to explore this field. With this book, the plan is to share basics of programming automated lighting fixtures while also providing useful information for those who have been working with this technology for several years. Much of this information comes from my own experience and knowledge. In addition, many esteemed programmers and designers have been consulted to ensure the data is accurate and timely.

Because this book is a guide strictly on the process of programming, which is essentially the same regardless of the fixture and console types, there is no mention of specific manufacturer's fixtures or consoles (except in the Appendix). Specific console syntax and fixture operations can be studied via the user's manuals provided by equipment manufacturers. The basic principles presented within this book apply to past, current, and future lighting technologies.

Programming automated lights is very much an art. Just as most anyone can learn to hold a paintbrush and put the paint on a canvas, the actual entering of data into a lighting console is fairly simple. The real art comes from years of experience, fine-tuning the procedures for painting the canvas or programming the console. Similar to painting, there is no right or wrong way to program, only the requirement to get the data into the desk in a method that produces the best show possible given all the constraints.

If you have ever wanted to know what goes on at the lighting console, or have a desire to become an automated lighting programmer, then please read on and enjoy.

10 Things Every Programmer Should Know

There are many things that every automated lighting programmer just ought to know. These basic concepts and routines help to create the groundwork for any production's lighting. A solid understanding of the following should help anyone interested in programming moving lights. The following is presented in no particular order:

#1–UNDERSTANDING THE FIXTURES

When starting with a new rig, you should first find out as much as you can about the fixtures you will have. Download the manuals and read up on the features and functions of the lights. Study the digital multiplexing (DMX) protocol so you understand what happens with different DMX values. A good understanding of how the fixture responds to DMX (and what is available) will aid in any programming. In addition, studying the different modes and options of the fixtures can result in optimal settings for your production.

#2 – BASIC CONSOLE OPERATIONS

Of course, if you do not know much about your console, how can you be expected to program it? You do not need to be a full fledged expert on every aspect of the desk (although this does not hurt), but at the very least you must be able to patch, create cues, recall cues, and backup the data.

#3 – PATCHING AND ADDRESSING

Once you have studied the fixtures and grasped your console, it is essential that you know how to connect the two together. Properly patching the desk and addressing the fixtures is a skill every programmer must possess. The more information you can provide to the crew about the patch, the better. Too often I have seen productions where the programmer did not create a patch until he was on-site and everyone was waiting around for the information.

#4 – MAKING LIGHTS MOVE

The most basic function you should be able to accomplish is to move fixtures from point A to point B using a repeatable method. Generally this requires two cues, one with the fixtures in position A and the other with the fixtures in position B. Then by crossfading between the two cues, the fixtures will move at the selected crossfade speed. You can then apply these procedures to the other parameters of your fixtures.

#5 – LONG HOURS AND LATE NIGHTS

Our industry often gives the lighting team the late night shift, so you must be prepared to spend many long nights at the console. Knowing how to prepare your body and mind for hours of staring at one canvas, while helping to create multiple paintings, is essential.

#6 – SUBTRACTIVE VERSUS ADDITIVE COLOR MIXING

The most common color mixing in moving lights uses three graduated dichroic filters: cyan, magenta, and yellow. By combining the three you can create millions of colors. This is usually called subtractive color mixing because you are removing (or filtering) wavelengths or colors out of white light. As more wavelengths are subtracted, the color tends to move closer to black. On the other hand, additive color mixing is generally accomplished by adding several sources together to get closer to white. For example, many of the new light emitting diode (LED) fixtures use additive color mixing by combining red, green, and blue sources.

#7 – TRACKING

Conventional lighting desks commonly record all values for all channels into every cue. Moving light consoles make use of tracking by recording only channels with changed values into each cue. This significantly reduces the amount of data in each cue and enables many tricks for dynamic programming and playback.

#8 – PROTECT THE DATA

A good programmer will protect the data in the console with his or her life. You are hired to enter the data into the console, and to see that it remains there (or can be recalled) at all times. Proper saving routines are essential as well as requiring an uninterruptible power supply (UPS) and a dedicated power source. If something goes wrong and all data is lost and you have no options for recovery, then only you are to blame.

#9 – HOW TO ADMIT YOUR FAULTS

If a Lighting Designer (LD) asks for a particular effect or look and you are unsure of how to create it, admit it. Do not tell the LD that it is not possible, either find a way to make it happen or tell him you do not know how to do it. One LD has told me of a time when his programmer said the console could not select fixtures based on their current color. The LD told him it was possible as his last programmer did it all the time. Again the programmer said it was not possible and told the LD he must be mistaken. The LD called his last programmer and had him explain to the current programmer how to do the function. Needless to say the LD never wanted to hire this guy again, although things would have been different if he had just admitted that he did not know how to perform the function.

#10 – WHO TO CALL

Write down the support phone numbers for all the lighting manufacturers and keep this with you at all times. Then when a problem develops, or when you need to know how to do something, call for assistance. Do not call instead of picking up a manual and trying to figure it out, but do call once you have exhausted other methods. In addition, there are many people in this industry who like to share their knowledge. Get to know others and network. I know of a group of programmers that try to get together once a month just to share experiences and problems with each other. This way they can all learn from one another.

BUT WAIT, THERE'S MORE

Sure, there is plenty more you need to know to be a successful automated lighting programmer. This book is filled with many of the basic concepts that are important to get you started. The most important thing to remember is that you are working on one element of the show, and to strive to make your part of it the best it can be for the overall production.

Programming Philosophies

The automated lighting programmer must have many skills beyond knowledge of simple programming syntax. The position requires one to evaluate each situation to determine the right method of operation. Some productions hire a programmer to handle all aspects of the lighting, while others hire a programmer to bring an LD's vision to life. Real world experience with many productions is the only way an automated lighting programmer can become successful. Knowledge, speed, accuracy, people skills, etc. are all vitally important, but there is no substitute for experience.

THE AUTOMATED LIGHTING PROGRAMMER

There are many different levels of productions, each requiring specific types of people on the production staff. Understandably there are several different categories of automated lighting programmers. Each holds an important position within our industry, by providing different levels of experience and knowledge.

First there is the **Weekend Warrior.** This type of person simply programs lights for fun, but has another main profession. They have little to no interest in learning more about the profession.

Next is the **Amateur Programmer.** They program lighting when and where they can (schools, churches, clubs, raves, etc.), but programming is not their main source of income. They have an interest in the profession and strive to learn more about automated lighting programming.

The **Apprentice Programmer** is involved in the lighting industry and programs whenever there is an opportunity. Oftentimes they are hired to work on productions in other positions than lighting programming (technician, followspot operator, etc.). They have a desire to gain as much programming experience and comprehension as possible.

A **Professional Programmer** earns his or her living by programming automated lighting. The majority of this person's income is from programming (80–90%). Automated lighting programming is their chosen career and they continue to study and improve their skills as much as possible.

Finally, the **Professional Programmer/Designer** works regularly as either a lighting programmer or lighting designer. Oftentimes this person will be hired onto a production filling both rolls simultaneously. The income of this professional will be split between programming and design. Continued improvement of knowledge and experience is continually sought by this career type.

Of course, like most jobs in the entertainment industry, some people will work on high-profile productions (award shows, Broadway, large tours, television shows, etc.) and get lots of press. Their names will be well known in the industry and they will be mentioned in magazines and on websites. Others will do many shows, but not be well recognized within the industry. Yet these individuals will still be successful programmers with a grand career.

THE HOLLYWOOD SYNDROME

Our industry is only a small part of "show business", yet it still lives up to many of the clichés. Many students and apprentices of the profession expect a fast track to the "big" shows. They see the concert tours roll through town and the live television broadcasts and think, "I can do that." Oftentimes these people will begin working with a lighting company and not understand why they are not going out on the next Michael Jackson tour as the programmer.

There is a good reason you see the same programmer's names on all the big shows: experience. While anyone can learn which buttons to press on a console, it takes many years of programming to learn how to get the most out of your fixtures, work with different types of productions and LDs, and handle any situation that is thrown at you. Ultimately the actual data in the console is not what is important, but rather the end result. If you were able to create the LD's vision in a timely manner and write the cue so that it is repeatable, then the methods of the data creation and storage are not essential.

Recently I was hired to program a live television special. The LD hired me because we have worked together before and he knows that I will come into the event and simply do my job. I have learned from my experiences not to wait for him on every detail of the show. He knows I will create original looks that fit with his style and work for the television camera. In fact he even told me that he is not worried about what patterns are in the fixtures, as he knows that I will "work my magic and create new visual images." If I had only programmed one or two shows in my life, he would not want to hire me for this production. There is an extremely short amount of time from load in to taping and he has no time to sit with a programmer to describe every bit of the show. So do not be in a hurry to jump into the "big shows." Instead, take your time and work hard and the large productions will come to you. You will learn more about lighting on every production you are involved with and should enjoy all the new challenges.

CREATIVITY AND CONSISTENCY

Usually lighting programmers are hired not only to assist in the creation and storage of an LD's vision, but also to share in the creative process. It is extremely important that an automated lighting programmer is both left and right brained. It is often said that one side of the brain is technical and the other creative. A programmer must be able to derive original looks, concepts, chases, etc. and then utilize the tools at hand to bring these ideas to life. Whether you are a highly creative person or not, there are many books and exercises on the subject of creativity. I strongly recommend exercising your brain as much as possible.

The technical side of a programmer's brain must contain the data needed to properly use a console and fixtures. In addition, regular, consistent routines should be used in console setup. For example, if you always number your colors or positions in a particular order, then no matter what show or console you are using you will know that Color 3 Position 5 equals "Down Center Stage Red." Do not just randomly layout your console with each show. Of course, there will be things specific to each production, but if your basic building blocks are the same your programming will be much faster and efficient.

LEARNING TO PROGRAM

Recently while in Tokyo, Japan enjoying many of their fine foods with friends, we discussed the puffer fish (fugu). If the puffer fish is not properly prepared, then it can lead to Tetrodotoxin poisoning which has a 50% mortality rate. In Japan only specially licensed sushi chefs are allowed to prepare and serve this dish. In fact, the Food and Drug Administration (FDA) allows properly prepared portions of the puffer fish into the United States only 2–3 times a year. The FDA's agreement with Japan states, "Experience has shown that the best method for obtaining a product which will not cause illness or death is the highly specialized training and knowledge for product preparation." Although an extreme analogy, automated lighting should not be taken lightly.

Luckily the mortality rate for improper programming of automated lights is extremely small, although I know some LDs who have wanted to kill their programmers! However, lighting programmers must practice their craft and continue to learn more. Consoles are always improving, new fixtures are released, and creative visions change. There are many resources to learn how to program, but practice makes perfect.

Look for Opportunities

Instead of waiting for the next gig to hone your skills, you need to find other avenues. The first place to look is your local lighting shop. Many companies will be willing to allow you to come to the shop and use a desk. While they may or may not have fixtures for you to plug in, at least you can use the console. And, as a bonus, when you are hanging out at the shop, you might just get offered a gig. If you can get your hands on a desk, build a practice show from scratch with cues and everything. Do not just sit in front of the desk and poke around. Put yourself into a real world situation and complete the required tasks.

If you do not have access to a console, you can always make use of offline editors. Most automated lighting consoles have applications for the personal computer (PC) that emulate the desk. Using this software you can practice the syntax and procedures of the console. In addition, many of the offline editors now either include visualization or work with popular visualization software on the same machine. This means you can sit at home and program virtual lights on a virtual console with your real computer.

Programming Exercises

The main reason to exercise your programming skills is so that the console functions become second nature, allowing you to spend more time being creative. When you do not have to think about how the console works, an amazing ability comes through. You find yourself simply commanding the fixtures to create the desired looks without thinking of how to enter the data into the console. Of course, there will be times that you will be challenged by the console, but the more comfortable you are with the programming syntax, the better.

There are many types of exercises you can do and I will suggest my favorite. Put yourself into the following scenario. You have been hired to program the lighting for a small 2-day business meeting using about 20 fixtures. Late in the first day the client surprises you by informing you a band will play during the lunch break the next day (a one hour period). They want you to "do lighting" for the band. It is now 7 P.M. and you can only be in the venue until 10 P.M. So you have 3 hours to program lighting for a band that you know nothing about (not even what type of music).

The exercise is to program 20 fixtures for 2–3 hours to prepare for this surprise. Then ask a friend to grab a mixed collection of compact disks (CDs). Have them randomly select a CD and song and play it for you. Playback your programming to the music. Then have them randomly select another CD and song and playback to that one. Keep doing this for about an hour and you will find out if you prepared yourself (and your desk) for anything that might come up. I find this exercise to be very consistent with real-world situations where you have to program and operate lighting for acts you have never seen or heard.

Explore Your World

A large part of being a good programmer and operator has nothing to do with the console. Your timing, rhythm, listening, visualization, and many other skills are just as important. Many of us often can't help but imagine lighting cues while listening to music, but how often do you really listen to the beat, changes, etc.? Instead of trying to visualize the actual lighting look, try just thinking about when to trigger the different cues.

Learn to anticipate changes in the music and recognize musical elements. Listen to all types of music, not just what you like. Even though your production may not contain musical elements, these skills will come in handy in most situations.

You can also exercise your mind by trying to think of ways to recreate natural lighting conditions. Pay attention to how the quality and color of light changes during a sunset or sunrise. One day watch a sunset on the horizon for 20 minutes, then next day watch a sunset on the side of a building or a tree. Sit in a dark house during a lightning storm paying attention to Mother Nature's lighting chases. These exercises will pay off even if you do not recreate these actual situations on stage, because they might inspire you to create an effect in a different manner.

Never Stop Learning

Just when you think you have mastered a console, think again. There is always something new to learn. Talk with others to see how they accomplish certain functions. Also try doing things in different ways. For example, if your desk has a very strong effects package, try building a simple 30-step chase "old school" style. You will find yourself someday in a situation where an LD wants an exact look that cannot be created using effects. For example, while I was working on an ice skating show the LD asked for a very specific chase. I thought I could build it with effects and he thought it would have to be programmed as a chase. We were ahead in our programming schedule, so he gave me the time to try to create it with the effects. He was correct and it was not possible. I then quickly built the chase as a 90-step cuelist and it did just as he wanted. Luckily I had the experience and knowledge to create this monster chase in a hurry.

Be an Artist

There is a true art to programming automated lights. It is a skilled craft that requires many years of experience to fully master the possibilities. Because every production has its own unique challenges and requirements, the programmer must be fully confident in his or her abilities with the console and fixtures. Yes, we are part of the creative arts, but we also perform a highly technical job. Just as a fine sushi chef must train for years to perfect the slicing of a puffer fish, we must maintain a high level of craftsmanship for our profession.

2

Automated Lighting Concepts

Before studying the practice of programming automated lights, you should be familiar with specific concepts associated with automated lighting. Having a good understanding of the principles involved will open the doors to better programming. The following topics provide a basic understanding of the most important concepts related to automated lighting programming.

DMX-512

Most automated lighting fixtures use a common language known as DMX-512. This standard signal specification allows for 512 discreet channels of control per data line or universe. Each of these control channels has the potential to be any value from 0 to 255. Originally designed for controlling dimmers, zero was mapped to 0% intensity and 255 was mapped to 100% intensity with a linear dispersion of all values in between. Generally this is still the case with dimmers, but DMX is also used by automated lighting fixtures. Each parameter of a fixture (pan, tilt, gobos, color mixing, etc.) is assigned a particular DMX channel. As the value for this channel changes, it will affect the specific function of the fixture. For instance, a gobo channel might assign no gobo at a value of zero, while a value of 25 will output the first gobo. A value of 50 will output the second gobo and a value of 75 the third. This mapping will continue through all 256 values of the DMX channel. The mappings of DMX channels to their functions for a specific fixture is known as the DMX protocol of the fixture.

DMX PROTOCOLS

The DMX protocol of a fixture is the mappings of parameters to specific DMX channels (see Table 2.1). For example, if a fixture uses 8 channels of DMX, channels 1 through 4 might be used for pan and tilt (some parameters such as pan and tilt use 2 DMX channels each for a finer resolution of control which is also known as 16-bit), 5 for dimmer, 6 for gobos, 7 for color, and 8 for shutter. Each individual fixture of this type needs to use 8 unique DMX channels within the universe total of 512 channels. The first channel each fixture uses (of its 8) is known as the fixture's DMX start channel, or DMX address of the fixture. When using three of these fixtures, you will need to address them at 1, 9, and 17, and will be using DMX channels 1 through 24 to control them.

FIXTURE MODES

Not all fixture protocols are created equal. A fixture might have different modes that allow various functions of the fixture. For example, a 16-channel wash light might have a 14-channel mode, a 16-channel mode with normal functions, a 16-channel mode with special functions, and an 18-channel advanced mode. It is very important to choose the mode that will provide the functionality you need for your show. Then each fixture must be set to this mode via its menu system or dipswitches. Most automated lighting consoles make use of fixture libraries that assign the programming features of the desk to the proper DMX channels for the fixture. When patching you must make sure the fixture library you use in the desk matches the mode assigned to the fixture. If you use the 14-channel mode library in the desk, but assign the fixture to the 16-channel mode, you will have problems controlling your lights. It is essential that you study the protocols of the fixture as well as the fixture libraries of your desk to ensure that not only do they match up, but that they also provide the functionality you desire.

Table 2.1 Sample DMX Protocol

DMX Channel	Purpose	Ranges
1	Pan Coarse	0–255
2	Pan Fine	0–255
3	Tilt Coarse	0–255
4	Tilt Fine	0–255
5	Intensity	0–255 (0 is no output and 255 is full output)
6	Gobo Wheel	0–10 no gobo
		11–30 gobo 1
		31–50 gobo 2
		51–70 gobo 3
		71–90 gobo 4
		91–110 gobo 5
		111–130 gobo 1 shake
		131–150 gobo 2 shake
		151–170 gobo 3 shake
		171–190 gobo 4 shake
		191–210 gobo 5 shake
		211–230 gobo wheel spin clockwise (linear)
		231–255 gobo wheel spin counterclockwise (linear)
7	Color Wheel	0 no color
		1–20 no color + 1 (linear)
		20 color 1
		21–39 color 1 + 2 (linear)
		40 color 2
		41–59 color 2 + 3 (linear)
		60 color 3
		61–79 color 3 + 4 (linear)
		80 color 4
		81–99 color 4 + 5 (linear)
		100 color 5
		101–110 color 5 + no color (linear)
		111–130 color 1 shake
		131–150 color 2 shake
		151–170 color 3 shake
		171–190 color 4 shake
		191–210 color 5 shake
		211–230 color wheel spin clockwise (linear)
		231–255 color wheel spin counterclockwise (linear)
8	Shutter	0–10 closed
		11–90 periodic strobes (varied speeds)
		91–150 random strobes (varied speeds)
		151–200 random synchronized strobes (varied speeds)
		200–220 fixture reset (hold for 10 seconds)
		221–230 lamp on (hold for 10 seconds)
		231–240 lamp off (hold for 10 seconds)
		241–255 open

CROSSFADE

When programming a lighting console, values are sent to specific DMX channels for controlling the fixtures. For example, if you program a fixture so it is color mixed to a green color, the console will assign values to Cyan at 255 and Yellow at 255. Now if you want to dissolve to yellow, you will need to change the cyan value to 0. By assigning a crossfade time to the change of cyan from 255 to 0, you will cause the console to send all values between 255 and 0 over the period of time specified. This linear change of values is known as a crossfade.

BUMP

A value change with a time of zero is known as a bump or snap change. If in the above example the crossfade time was set to 0, then the console would instantly change the DMX value of the cyan channel from 255 to 0 without sending any other values. This would result in an instantaneous change from green to yellow.

PARAMETER ABILITIES

Some fixture parameters are fully crossfadable, while others allow for only snap changes. By reading the DMX protocol provided by the manufacturer, you can determine if a function is crossfadable. Generally a continually variable parameter (linear) can be crossfaded, while a parameter with indexed values will not be crossfadable. Looking at the sample DMX protocol (see Table 2.1), one can see that the gobo values are indexed and not crossfadable. Because each gobo has a range of values assigned to the full gobo, crossfading from 51 to 75 will cause the fixture to snap from gobo 3 to gobo 4. Crossfading is possible with the color wheel because the DMX ranges allow for linear positioning of the color wheel. Crossfading from 40 to 60 will scroll from color 2 to color 3 on the color wheel.

PRECEDENCE (HTP AND LTP)

When an automated lighting console changes the values of a parameter for a fixture, usually the most recent change has the highest priority. For example, if the first cue points a fixture to stage right, then the second cue moves the fixture to stage left, this new value for pan and tilt takes precedence over the previous value. This type of priority is known as latest takes precedence (LTP) because the latest change will affect the fixtures regardless of the value sent to it. LTP is generally used by automated lighting consoles for all parameters of fixtures.

Some lighting consoles have an option of using highest takes precedence (HTP) for intensity parameters. In this case, the value closer to 255 will have priority over a lower value. For instance, cue one has an intensity of 80% (DMX value 205) and cue two has an intensity of 50% (DMX value 128). When using HTP, cue one will have priority over cue two and the fixture will remain at 80% because cue one has a higher value than cue two. Highest takes precedence is extremely useful to ensure that conventional channels are not accidentally blacked out or dimmed down by other cues. HTP is generally used only for intensity channels as most other parameters are not as clearly defined at specific values (i.e., greater value = more output).

TRACKING

Most automated lighting consoles use a process called tracking. To a seasoned programmer, tracking is an essential tool. However, for those without a complete understanding of tracking, it often works against them.

Nontracking Consoles

To better explain tracking, I will first describe how a nontracking console works. As an example, I have a show with six fixtures and am building cue one. After assigning the intensity to full, each fixture is moved to its desired position and the color is adjusted. Then this information is stored as cue one. My console will save not only the changes I made to the fixtures (intensity, position, and color) but also all the other attribute settings for the fixtures. The cue contains data that tells my fixtures not only where to point and in which color, but also which color to project, which iris setting, etc. (see Figure 2.1).

When building cue two simply move the fixtures to a new position; again my console will record data for all parameters of the fixtures (see Figure 2.2). While building cue two I have to assign the fixtures to the

NON-TRACKING CONSOLE							CUE 1
	Dim	Pan	Tilt	Color	Gobo	Iris	Shutter
1	100	75	32	Red	Open	100	Open
2	100	87	55	Red	Open	100	Open
3	100	20	52	Red	Open	100	Open
4	100	15	45	Red	Open	100	Open
5	100	84	100	Red	Open	100	Open
6	100	41	22	Red	Open	100	Open

Figure 2.1 Nontracking Console Cue One Example

same settings as cue one or I will see unexpected changes when going to cue two (the color assigned in cue one will revert back to the console defaults in cue two).

Usually to avoid this problem, the programmer will copy cue one to cue two, then make the needed changes to cue two. This creates a problem when you want to change the color used in cues 1–6. You will have to edit all six cues because each cue has the same color information. This is where tracking saves the day.

Tracking Consoles

As stated above, nontracking consoles store values for all parameters of all fixtures in each and every cue. A tracking console will *only* store the

NON-TRACKING CONSOLE							CUE 2
	Dim	Pan	Tilt	Color	Gobo	Iris	Shutter
1	100	32	75	Red	Open	100	Open
2	100	55	87	Red	Open	100	Open
3	100	52	20	Red	Open	100	Open
4	100	45	15	Red	Open	100	Open
5	100	100	84	Red	Open	100	Open
6	100	22	41	Red	Open	100	Open

Figure 2.2 Nontracking Console Cue Two Example

values of the parameters you have adjusted. In simple terms, tracking avoids redundant data in the cuelist. Using the same example, build cue one by assigning intensity, position, and color. When this information is stored as cue one, my console will only save the changes made to the fixtures (see Figure 2.3). My cue contains only the intensity, position, and color settings and no other information.

Now as cue two is being built, I again simply move the fixtures to a new position and save the changes (see Figure 2.4). All other settings for the fixture (color, color, iris, etc.) will track into cue two from the previous cue(s).

If I want to change the color being used in cues 1–6, then I will only need to edit cue one as the color setting will track into the following cues.

Advantages of Tracking

When working with one large cuelist or cue stack, tracking has many advantages. First, cue creation is very easy. If cue two only needs to move the fixtures to stage right, then this is the only information needed in cue two. There is no need to copy the other parameter settings from cue one. Secondly, because the console is only storing the changes made to each cue, editing becomes much simpler. For example, if you have thirty cues in a row with the intensity of your fixtures at 100%, this intensity setting only needs to be stored in the first cue. All the subsequent cues can be written with no value for intensity. The 100% setting will track through all 30 cues until you change the intensity on cue 31 to 0%. Later if you

	Dim	Pan	Tilt	Color	Gobo	Iris	Shutter	CUE 1
1	100	75	32	Red				
2	100	87	55	Red				
3	100	20	52	Red				
4	100	15	45	Red				
5	100	84	100	Red				
6	100	41	22	Red				

TRACKING CONSOLE

Figure 2.3 Tracking Console Cue One Example

TRACKING CONSOLE							
	Dim	Pan	Tilt	Color	Gobo	Iris	Shutter	CUE 2
1		32	75					
2		55	87					
3		52	20					
4		45	15					
5		100	84					
6		22	41					

Figure 2.4　Tracking Console Cue Two Example

decide to change the intensity level for cues 1–30 you will only need to edit cue one as the setting tracks through all the other cues.

Another powerful advantage to tracking is the ability to build cues or chases that only affect certain parameters or fixtures. This is the magic that allows programmers to assign to a bump button a cue that will strobe the fixtures without changing any other parameters. At any point in a show the bump button can be pressed to add strobing to the fixtures without changing any other parameter settings. On a nontracking console this would not be possible as the cue assigned to the bump button would have to contain position, color, etc. as well as strobe.

Disadvantages of Tracking

As you have read, tracking is very beneficial; however, it can also be confusing and frustrating. Back to my first example above, when building cue one only the changes (intensity, position, and color) were recorded, not any color, iris, etc. values. When creating the cue the fixture had no color, but this information was not recorded because no changes were made to the color parameter. Later when running the show this cue is played back and mysteriously a color is projecting on stage. This can happen when another cuelist is played prior to my example cuelist. Because cue one had no data for the color parameter, the console tracked the previous color setting into cue one. The solution to this problem is to edit cue one so it contains color data, telling the fixture to project no color in cue one. The same problem can occur in reverse when another cue is playing as a new cue is built. If an active cuelist assigns the fixtures to red and a new cue is written with no color information stored, then the fixtures may or may not be red when the new cue is played back. If a different cue is played first assigning your fixtures to green, then the green will track into this new cue. This is because your new cue will allow any previous color to track into it.

In my example regarding 30 cues with the intensity at 100%, a different tracking problem could develop. If cues 1–15 are for one dance number and cues 16–30 are for another then you change the intensity in cue one to 85%, you have just changed the intensity level for two different portions of your show. A good programmer will ensure that when edits are made, they do not track into subsequent cues where the changes are not desired. In Chapter 5, I will describe a very useful tool to solve this type of error, the block cue.

Practice Makes Perfect

Tracking is often considered one of the hardest concepts for automated lighting programmers to grasp. The results of tracking are often bewildering to the novice, as the console appears to not playback what was recorded. With an understanding of tracking, a programmer can manipulate the features of most automated lighting consoles with ease. The best method to ensure your understanding is with practice, so fire up your console and practice programming with tracking.

There are many fundamental concepts related to automated lighting programming. Each fixture and console may refer to these items using different terminology, but a good programmer will identify the similarities and easily adapt to the specific vocabulary. With a basic understanding of these ideas you are ready to learn the particulars of automated lighting programming.

3

Preparing for Programming

There are many things that must be taken into consideration before you can begin programming. In many ways a lighting programmer is similar to an airline pilot. We are at the controls of very sophisticated equipment, often working to meet impossible deadlines, and usually not seen by the audience (passengers). Just as a pilot will not simply board a plane and take off, most automated lighting programmers do not just walk up to a console and rig and begin entering cues into the desk. There is a certain amount of preparation that must be completed prior to taking off and building cues. Once the cues are built, an efficient saving routine must be followed to ensure all the hard work is protected.

FIXTURE SETUP

Before the lighting rig is set up, you need to be sure to communicate a few things to the crew. Programming will proceed smoothly if the fixtures are all hanging in the same direction (where applicable). If you have a batten with six wash lights on it you want to make sure all the fixtures are oriented in the same direction. If two of them are 180 degrees off from the others, then when you tilt them all together, four of them will move upstage and two will move downstage. In addition, as most fixtures use wheels to bring in colors and effects, if they are facing different directions, these wheels will appear to be coming from different sides of the stage. The best method to ensure the fixtures are facing the same direction is to place them all with their LEDs or data cables pointing in the identical direction.

We live in an age when software makes everything function. Fixture manufacturers continually upgrade their fixture software to make improvements and add features. If your fixtures have different versions of operating software, then they might behave differently. For example, a hard edge fixture might have an update to its software allowing the gobos to rotate at a faster rate. If two of your fixtures have an older version, then they will not be able to match the rest of the rig. Asking the crew to ensure that all fixtures have the most current operating software before the rig is assembled will help reduce problems later on.

Most fixtures have a method of inverting pan and or tilt via dip-switches or menus. Likewise most moving light consoles have the ability to assign these settings from the console. It is best to have the crew turn off all pan and tilt inverts at the fixtures and allow the console to perform this function. If the function is assigned at the fixture, then this setting must be remembered if the fixture is ever taken down and replaced. If there is a general rule that all fixtures have pan and tilt settings set to off then the chance of error is reduced. In addition, some fixtures may have additional settings to allow for faster color changes or mirror movements. Once again you will want to assign all fixtures the same settings; otherwise, problems will develop as you program.

THE CONSOLE

As the programmer, you are responsible for the operation of your console. You should be aware of not only how the console functions, but also what is required for your production. For instance, if you are going to use the Society of Motion Picture and Television Engineers (SMPTE) timecode, you will need to specify to the sound crew what type of connector is required for the console's input. In addition, you need to be aware of the version of software loaded in the desk. If you simply turn on the console and begin programming, you might find the console's fixture library does not contain the fixtures you need or, even worse, you might run into some console bugs. Just as fixture manufacturers are continually updating their software, so are the console manufacturers. I always go to the website of the console manufacturer and download the latest software as well as the list of changes and/or bug fixes. I then read all the documentation and determine if upgrading will be beneficial. Many programmers find a version of software they are comfortable with and do not upgrade beyond it until absolutely required. Remember everyone on the show will be looking at you when something goes wrong with the console, so you should load the version of software you think is best. Good programmers carry with them the version of software they intend to use on the console and do not count on the lighting supplier to have the console preloaded with whichever version. It is also good practice to not change console operating software during the run of a show unless absolutely necessary (for example, bug fixes). Wait until next season to upgrade and follow that old saying, "if it ain't broke, don't fix it".

When specifying the console, you should also specify what accessories you will need. Never assume the lighting provider will supply a keyboard, trackball, monitors, etc. If you intend to have video graphics array (VGA) monitors to connect to the console, be sure to place them on the order. If you know that production table space is at a premium, you might need to ask for flat screen monitors to save space. It is best if you can plug the console into an UPS and have additional front of house (FOH) power for anything else you might need (laptops, cell phone chargers, etc.). In addition, make sure that nothing else gets plugged into the UPS except the console. You do not want the LD's coffeepot killing the power to the desk in the middle of programming. Speaking of which, the FOH area often becomes your home during the production period. I always ask for a comfortable chair or stool, as I do not want to sit on a road case for a week (or even one day). There is nothing worse than being uncomfortable 14 hours a day. Other items you might need at FOH include floppy disks, little lights, audio playback (jam box), and/or video equipment (see Table 3.1).

Many productions require a backup console. Usually the console will be loaded with the final show files and be standing by in case something happens to the main console. In some cases an A/B switch is used to toggle the DMX lines should the master console go down. Oftentimes the testing of the backup console gets put off till just before it is needed. On the day of load in, it is important to open the box of the backup and test to make sure it can load and save a show. This way if you ever need to change out, you know it is in working order. When presented with the need for full redundant tracking backups, be sure to test all Musical Instrument Digital Interface (MIDI) or Ethernet connections to ensure the tracking is functioning properly prior to the programming period.

Table 3.1   Suggested Front of House Items

Monitors	Backup Console	Intercom	Coffee Pot/Cooler with Ice
Keyboard	Floppy Disks or CDs	Power (multiple circuits)	Trash Can
Mouse/ Trackball	Little Lights	Production Monitor(s) (for televised productions)	Chair(s) and Table(s)
UPS	Audio/Video Playback	Printer	Barricades/Security Personnel

Most consoles require a certain amount of setup before you can begin programming. While the rig is going up, take the time to create screen views, layouts, macros, etc. In addition, go through the other setup options to define other specific options you need for your show such as SMPTE or MIDI. Prepare as much as you can before arriving at the show site. Either use a console in the shop, or the offline editing software of your console for preparations.

PREPARING THE PATCH

One of the first things that must happen when preparing a show is patching the console. If the patch is incorrect, then the console will be unable to communicate properly with the fixtures. Most fixtures communicate via DMX-512, the universal lighting language. Within this network of data each fixture is assigned a DMX start address that must be entered into the console. Sometimes the fixture addressing will be determined prior to the patching, sometimes the patching will dictate the addressing. This will depend upon the size of the show, the crew chief, the LD, and the programmer. Even before you begin patching you have to understand how DMX addressing works.

Let's say you have a rig of 6 hard edge fixtures and 6 wash fixtures. The hard edge fixtures each use 18 channels of DMX and the wash fixtures 16 each. This means you will be using a total of 204 DMX channels. You now need to determine the start address for each fixture. There are two ways to calculate this. One way is to sit down with a notepad and calculator and do the math. The other method is to patch them into your console or its offline editor (see Table 3.2). I prefer to use the console

Table 3.2 Sample DMX Patch

User Number	Fixture Type	DMX Starting Address
1	Hard Edge	1
2	Hard Edge	19
3	Hard Edge	37
4	Hard Edge	55
5	Hard Edge	73
6	Hard Edge	91
11	Wash	109
12	Wash	125
13	Wash	141
14	Wash	157
15	Wash	173
16	Wash	189

method, as most consoles do not allow overlapping addresses (they do not allow for mistakes that could be made with a paper and pen). Also, once the information is in the desk, you can print the patch and use the printout to address the fixtures correctly.

If the desk is capable of more than one universe of DMX, then fixtures can be placed on the different universes. For example, if you have fixtures on the truss and fixtures on the floor, you might want to run a separate data line to each location. You could then plug the truss fixtures into universe 1 and the floor fixtures into universe 2. Since each universe is its own set of 512 DMX channels, you can address your fixtures within their own unique universe. So you might have two fixtures with the same DMX address, but on different universes. Of course, if you have a large number of fixtures in your rig, then you will have to make use of the different universes.

It does not take long to utilize all 512 channels, as most modern fixtures use 16 to 24 DMX channels. If your fixtures use 20 DMX channels each you can only patch 25 fixtures per universe (20 × 25 = 500). When determining the patch, you will want to make sure the point you change universes is a logical one. For instance, let's say you have a front truss and a back truss each with 15 fixtures using 20 channels each. You would not want to put 25 fixtures on one universe and 5 on the other, as one of the trusses would require two separate data runs (one for each universe). You would be better off to patch 15 fixtures to each universe and run one data line to each truss.

NUMBERS EVERYWHERE

Depending upon your desk, you might have a host of numbers assigned to your fixtures. Most consoles allow the programmer to define the "handle" for the fixture. The handle or user number is the number the programmer uses to select and program the fixture. This number is usually different than the actual DMX address of the fixture. This is because you generally want to number the fixtures in a linear order. In addition, you might choose to number them in a method that makes selecting them quicker and easier. One example would be to number the fixtures on the downstage truss 1–6 and the fixtures on the upstage truss 11–16. This way the user number reminds you of the placement of the fixture (downstage fixtures are less than 10 and upstage fixtures are greater than 11). Some programmers like to number according to fixture location, others according to fixture type. You might make the hard edge fixtures 21–28 and the wash fixtures 31–42. Another trick of the trade is to begin each sequence of numbering with the digit 1. For example, if I have 48 fixtures with 8 on each of 5 trusses, I might number them as 1–8, 11–18, 21–28, 31–38, and 41–48. You will notice I am not using the digits 10, 20, 30, and 40.

Most programmers find it easier to remember which fixture is which if they begin the numbering at 11, 21, 31, and 41. This is because we can look at any of the five trusses and quickly determine the first, second, third, fourth, etc. fixture. If we had to deal with a zero, it would be more confusing to glance at a piece of truss and select the fifth light from stage right.

Once all the user numbers are assigned and the fixtures are addressed, then the DMX addresses in the patch can be forgotten. As the programmer, you will only be working with the fixtures via their assigned handles. These numbers should be given to the LD and the crew so that everyone will refer to the fixtures via the same numbers. If you have a problem with fixture 85, you want the crew to know exactly which light you are talking about. When drawing a plot, you should put both the handles and the DMX address on the plot so that everyone can glance at the plot for the information they need (see Figure 3.1).

When working with an LD, it is important to decide who determines the handle numbering. Some LDs will dictate what the numbers

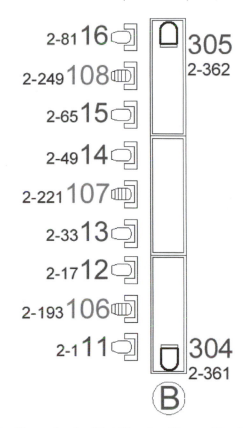

Figure 3.1 An Example of a Plot Showing Fixture Numbering and DMX Addressing

will be, but most allow the programmer to make this determination. In this case the programmer will need to notify the LD of the numbers that have been assigned. The LD can then enter these into the plot and paperwork and use the numbers when calling out cue data to the programmer.

After the patch is complete, it is time to test. If the fixtures are set up incorrectly, then the response from them will either be incorrect, erratic, or nonexistent. Once the entire rig appears to work, you need to check each fixture to ensure they are set to the correct address. If you simply select all fixtures at 100% to confirm they are working, you may not know that two of them have the same address. It is imperative that you cycle through each fixture one at a time to confirm they are responding to the correct user number and DMX address you have assigned in your patch. You might also cycle through all the gobos to make sure all fixtures have the correct patterns in the same slots (especially if the LD has requested custom patterns).

GROUPS

Once you have your console and fixtures operating correctly, the next step is to begin setting up the specific programming tools for your show. A good starting procedure is building fixture groups. A fixture group is a simple console function that allows for instant selecting of specific fixtures. Many moving light consoles will premake groups by fixture type (all brand x wash lights, even brand x wash lights, odd brand x wash lights), but there are many others you will want to create. Take a look at the show you are about to program and decide how you are going to break down the rig for quicker programming. For example, you might make a group with all hard edge fixtures on the upstage truss, another for the downstage truss, and another for the floor fixtures (see Table 3.3). By creating these groups prior to the programming session, you will be able to quickly select a bank of lights for specific programming purposes. In fact, many groups can be built using an offline editor or a desk in the shop.

PROTECTING YOUR WORK

As a moving light programmer, it is your duty to safeguard the lighting console data. I have seen consoles crash, show files become corrupt, floppy and hard disks fail, and even intentional sabotage. Lighting programmers must ensure that the data they create is protected so that the lighting of the show is not lost or damaged. Saving should happen from the moment the console preparation begins until after the final performance.

When you are hired to program a show, you are not just responsible for the entry of the data into the console, but also for the protection of

Table 3.3 Common Groups

All of each fixture type	Fixtures by location
Odd of each fixture type	All moving fixtures
Even of each fixture type	All conventional fixtures

that data. If data is lost due to console crashes, storage media failure, or operator error, it is up to the programmer to reenter all lost data. This can lead to a tremendous loss of time and creative energy. Of course, there are the rare instances where a cue can be built better the second time around, but usually you want to avoid having to rebuild cues. Lack of proper saving can add up to thousands of dollars for the producers. If reprogramming is required, someone has to pay the bills and this is one of the quickest ways to not get rehired.

The many consoles on the market use just a few methods of storing their data. Older controllers might use a random access memory (RAM) card, while newer consoles use hard drives, Zip disks, and even compact disc-rewritables (CDRWs) (see Figure 3.2). No matter the media, it is important to remember that all storage devices can fail at some point. Whichever media your console uses, you should always make multiple backups on various types of media. Even if your console has a hard drive and can make regular saves in the background, it is highly advised that you archive your work on other devices (floppy disk, CD, Zip, etc.).

It is very important to design a saving regimen that works for you and your console and stick to it so it becomes habit. For example, when

Figure 3.2 Various Forms of Media Used for Show Storage and Backup

I am programming a show, I will save my work on the native storage (hard drive or floppy) as well as make backups onto additional floppy disks. I then make off-site copies daily so I can refer back to any day's work.

Let's say the worst thing happens — your console crashes and erases everything since your last save. This could mean you have lost hours of work, unless you are diligent about saving often. For instance, you are working on a concert tour and you decide to save as you finish programming each song. If each song averages three hours of programming, then you will be in big trouble when data is lost. If you instead save several times during the three-hour period, then you will not feel so depressed when something goes wrong. Sometimes it can be difficult to follow this regimen as you and the LD will get into a rhythm and want to keep pressing forward. The longer you proceed without saving, the more you are living on the edge. Try to force yourself to make a point to save often (especially after creating a long sequence that was difficult to program). It is much better to wait a few minutes for the backup than to have to start over from scratch. Another rule I personally follow is to never walk away from a console without first saving the show. Whether I am going to the restroom or just up on stage for a moment, I will save my work to ensure that nothing occurs while I am away from the desk.

Now that you see the importance of saving often, there are more guidelines to follow. No matter the storage media, it is important to save to different files or disks. If you save often but always to the same floppy disk or the same file on your hard drive, then you are still living dangerously. What if that file or floppy becomes corrupted or fails? Then even with your diligent saving, your work could still be lost. For consoles that save directly to floppy disk without a hard-drive, I suggest the following "leapfrog" method of saving your show (see Figure 3.3). Start with 3–5 disks and label these A, B, C, D, and E. Stack them in alphabetical order. Each time you save, take the disk from the top of the stack and save your show. Then on the next save remove the current disk and place it on the bottom of the pile.

This way if something happens, you have 2 to 4 previous copies to refer to. If working with a console that uses a hard drive for storage, then save to different files on the hard drive. Try to name the file so you do not get confused as to which file is the latest (although you can usually read the time and date stamp of the saved file). For example, you might save your show files as "myshowA," "myshowB," "myshowC," etc. Also, it is a good idea to make periodic archives to another media besides the hard drive in the event of a hard drive failure.

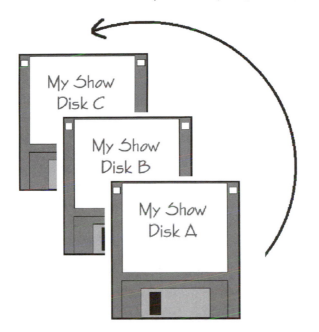

Figure 3.3   The "Leapfrog" Method of Data Storage

Once you have completed your programming session each day, it is very important to make and store multiple copies of your current show file. If you simply save it on the console and come back the next day, then what happens if the console lost your show file (or the console is missing, etc.)? I usually make 2 copies for myself (and keep my last 2 disks in the leapfrog set as well). In addition, I will make a copy for the LD and a copy for the crew chief. By distributing multiple copies of the show, I have ensured that should something happen to me (I walk though a highly magnetic zone or am hit by a truck, etc.) then someone else will still have a copy of the show data. Also, I will then make a copy of the show file onto my laptop when I return to my hotel room (or on-site if I have my laptop with me at the console). Making a separate folder on your computer for each day's work ensures you always have an older copy of the show to refer back to. Once the show is complete, you can delete all but the final show from your computer (unless you like to hang on to all that data).

Many programmers use even stricter methods of protecting their work. Think of your saving method as insurance. Spend as much time saving as you feel you can afford. Keep in mind that the more you spend the more you will be protected in the event of a catastrophe (but you do not want to spend all your time waiting for the desk to write to disk). I would not suggest saving after each cue is built, but I have seen programmers who save nearly as often. Some people will save thirty times a day to two boxes of disks and others will save five times to three disks. The most important choice is to find a saving method that works for you and to use it consistently.

ALWAYS BE PREPARED

Each new production you program will present its own unique challenges. This is one of the reasons that working as an automated lighting programmer can be so much fun. Proper preparation for each new endeavor will allow you the freedom and piece of mind to concentrate on making the current production the best it can be. From ensuring the fixtures are operating correctly to setting up the console in an efficient manner, every bit of preparation will undoubtedly help the show. Many moving light consoles will allow you to import your common palettes and setups to make some of the initial setup even easier.

In the future, when DMX is replaced by a network friendly protocol, each fixture might tell the desk what line it is plugged into and what its functions are. Then the programmer will only need to assign a user number to the fixture and begin programming. Some manufacturers have already incorporated this functionality using DMX via talkback and have consoles that can remotely address the fixtures according to the patch in the desk. However, for the foreseeable future programmers will have to patch their fixtures into the desk by hand as part of their normal preparations for a show.

By preparing for each production with proper planning for the front of house, fixtures, console setup, patch, and groupings, you can begin concentrating on your programming sooner. As the preparations become habit, you will find it a simple process to specify what is needed as well as to prebuild or import data into the console. Much of programming is about consistency and a consistent setup procedure helps produce an efficient programming experience.

4

Basic Programming

Programming automated lights is essentially the data entry of specialized instructions into a custom computer application. This data is then
transmitted via a unique protocol to robotic lighting fixtures. While this
appears as a simple process, there is much more involved than simple
data entry. An automated lighting programmer must be familiar with the
particulars of the lighting console, the fixtures, the production, and the
lighting designer. With a basic understanding of each of these elements,
a programmer is able to properly create the lighting programming
required for any production.

UNDERSTANDING YOUR FIXTURES

I can get inside my car and drive it to the airport; then I can get inside
a rental car at my destination and drive it with ease. The steering
wheel, gas, and brake pedals, etc. are all in the same location and have
the same functions as all other cars. In Australia I drove a right-hand-
drive car and had to learn the differences, but the elements still
worked the same (steering, braking, etc.). Moving light programming
generally is not as easy as driving a car. This is because there are no
standards when it comes to how fixture parameters should respond
to DMX.

Imagine if steering one car you just used the steering wheel, then another type of car you had to turn a knob to adjust the steering wheel mode between turning mode, straight mode, and skid mode. Yet another type of car required turning the steering wheel, adjusting the knob, and pressing on a pedal to adjust the speed of the turning. It would be very difficult to adjust from one vehicle to another, without first studying the method of steering. This is the case with many automated lighting functions!

Many hard-edged automated fixtures have rotating gobos. The number of DMX channels used to select and rotate a single gobo can range from 1 to 5 depending on fixture type and DMX mode. Because of all the differences, most lighting consoles simply apply the DMX protocols of the fixtures to adjustable parameters. This can lead to much confusion when programming as it requires the programmer to be familiar with the particularities of each fixture's protocol.

It is imperative that you study the DMX protocol of each fixture type within your lighting rig so you understand the capabilities and functions of that particular unit. Without this basic understanding, you will spend most of your time trying to figure out how to "drive" each fixture. Just because you know how to rotate gobos with one type of fixture does not mean you can do the same with others. Prior to beginning programming you should read the DMX protocol of each light and then test its functions. I suggest downloading the manuals and protocols of fixtures before you even arrive at the production site. In addition, you can use most console's offline editors to determine exactly how the fixtures are implemented into the console.

Although every fixture is different, there are some common guidelines as to how most professional automated lighting fixtures function. Below I have listed the common parameters and their usual functions. Please be aware that both console and fixture manuals might refer to these items with different terminology.

Pan and Tilt—Controls the movement of a mirror or moving head. Typically 2 channels are used for each parameter to create 16-bit accuracy.

Intensity—Usually 0–100% will control the output of the fixture. **Note**: some manufacturers place additional parameters on this channel such as strobe or control.

Color Mixing—Cyan, Magenta, and Yellow are variably controlled via 0–100%, with zero equal to no color and 100% full color. Some fixtures are reversed or will contain additional fixed colors on the same control channel.

Fixed Color—Certain values on this channel will recall specific colors from a color wheel. Other values may recall half or split colors. In addition there are usually premade spins of the color wheel at different speeds to select from this channel.

Frost—0–100% provides variable control of a frosting or softening of the output. Usually zero is equal to no frost and 100% full frost; however, some fixtures are reversed or may contain additional frost strobing effects.

Shutter Strobe—This channel will control the shutter of the fixture. The shutter will normally be open, with an option for closed. In addition, various types and speeds of strobing will be available. Some manufacturers also place control functions on this channel.

Control—The control channel often contains all nonstandard programming functions. Lamp on/off, fixture shutdown, fixture reset or home, and other specific functions are accessed from this channel. Usually a modifier (strobe channel closed) and/or a time value (hold at a value for 5 seconds) is required to prevent accidental triggering of control functions.

Fixed Gobo—Certain values on this channel will recall specific gobos from a nonrotating gobo wheel. Other values may recall half or partial gobos. In addition, there are usually premade spins and/or shakes of the gobo wheel at different speeds to select from this channel.

Rotating Gobo—Certain values on this channel will recall specific rotating gobos from a rotating gobo wheel. Other values may recall half or partial gobos. In addition, there are usually premade spins and/or shakes of the gobo wheel at different speeds to select from this channel.

Rotate Speed—Most manufacturers use an additional channel to adjust the speed of rotation for the rotating gobo wheel. Depending on the fixture, this channel might also select the mode (indexing, rotate forward or reverse) of the rotating gobo.

Iris—This channel will adjust the iris of the fixture from a small size to full open (or vice versa) when adjusted from 0–100%. In addition, the channel might include premade iris strobing and effects.

Speed—Many fixtures include speed channels to allow for fixture control crossfades of values. This functionality is used to create smoother transitions than is possible by most DMX controllers. See below for further information on speed channels.

Mode Channels—Sometimes a manufacturer will add mode channels to their fixtures. These channels are used to modify the functionality of another channel. For example, a color mode channel will change the behavior of the protocol for the fixed color wheel. The normal mode for the color wheel might be to select fixed colors as the value changes from

0–100%. If a different mode is selected from the color mode channel, it will change the fixed color channel so it will spin at various speeds from 0–100%. Yet another mode might spin the wheel the opposite direction, or allow for oscillating between two colors at different speeds. Mode channels are commonly found for color wheels, gobo wheels, and rotating gobos.

There are many more parameter types depending upon your fixture type. Refer to the fixture's DMX protocol documentation for exact details on all parameters. If you are unsure as to how a particular function is controlled from your lighting console, it is best to experiment with some test cues.

SPEED CHANNELS

DMX is a simple protocol that was developed to control lighting dimmers. As automated lighting developed, it latched onto this protocol as a uniform standard for lighting control. However the resolution offered by 256 values per channel is rather limiting. Most manufacturers found they needed a higher resolution for pan and tilt. By combining two DMX channels to control a single parameter, they are able to achieve 65,535 values per parameter. This is referred to as 16-bit DMX control and is commonly used for pan and tilt as well as rotating gobo indexing.

With very slow movements of fixture parameters, 256 or even 65,535 values are not enough. If you have ever tried to move a parameter extremely slowly (2 minutes or more), then you have probably noticed a shaky or steppy movement. This is because the resolution DMX crossfading is less than adequate in these situations. For this reason most manufacturers of automated lighting have provided a timing parameter to achieve higher resolution movements. Now instead of stepping between a value of 10 and 22 across 2 minutes via a DMX crossfade, you can tell the fixture to move from one position to another in 2 minutes smoothly. The console instantly sends the new value and speed timing to the fixture, and the fixture moves the parameter at the selected time with a much higher resolution than can be achieved via DMX. This usually results in smoother parameter movements.

So how do you use these magic-timing parameters? Well, that really depends upon your fixture, so it is back to reading the DMX protocol for you. First, however, you need to know what to look for as each manufacturer has different names and types of speed controls. Some of the names are Mspeed, Vector Speed, Beam Time, Focus Time, Color Time, Speed,

Vector, and Xfade. The names might be different, but there are some similarities in programming these timing functions.

The first rule is that if you are not going to use the timing functions, ensure that you have the channel(s) set to their off setting. This is not the same as the fastest speed setting, but a different value that disables the internal timing of the fixture altogether. The speed controls of fixtures are often broken down by type of parameter (beam, color, pan/tilt, etc.). On the other hand, some manufacturers provide one universal speed parameter and then allow the programmer to select which parameter will be affected by the speed channel. For example, the DMX protocol of the channel used for gobo selection might have all 6 gobos in crossfade mode and then all 6 gobos in speed mode (see Table 4.1).

Selecting gobo 2 from either section of the protocol will yield the same image on stage; however, the speed mode version will respond to the speed channel timing. When selected with speed timing on, the gobos will scroll into their position in a time defined by the speed channel. Without this setting the gobos will either jump directly to their new setting or follow the console's crossfade time. Always refer to the user's manual to see how specific fixtures function.

Table 4.1   Sample Gobo Channel DMX Protocol

DMX Channel	DMX Value	Effect
8 Gobo	0–10	Open
	11–30	Gobo 1
	31–40	Gobo 2
	41–60	Gobo 3
	61–80	Gobo 4
	81–100	Gobo 5
	101–120	Gobo 1 speed controlled
	121–140	Gobo 2 speed controlled
	141–160	Gobo 3 speed controlled
	161–180	Gobo 4 speed controlled
	181–200	Gobo 5 speed controlled
	201–240	Gobo spin varied speeds
	241–255	Open

If the desired effect is to change from one gobo to another in time of 2 minutes, you would select gobo 2 (possibly in speed mode), then set the speed channel (possibly the beam speed) to 2 minutes. Now you must ensure that your console does not try to crossfade the value for the gobo channel or the speed channel. The best thing to do is to assign the gobo channel and the speed channel a crossfade time of zero (or set the entire cue time to zero). If you were to crossfade either of these two parameters, you would confuse the fixture, as it would try to calculate the movement speed while the desk is crossfading. The result would be a movement much slower than you intended.

To avoid having a separate speed channel for each parameter of the fixture, the manufacturers have given us either one speed channel, or several categorized speed channels. This means that when you assign a gobo to change in two minutes, this might also affect other beam parameters or even pan and tilt. This is where you need to study the manual again to determine what options you have. Some fixtures have options on controls or other channels to disable speed functions from pan, tilt, etc. In addition, with tracking consoles you need to be aware of when you have turned on the speed channel. You might need to turn it off for the next cue. If you forget to turn it off, then it will remain on for the rest of your show and possibly wreak havoc with all your future crossfades. In addition, if you try to manually move the fixture or its parameters, it might take two minutes to change from one gobo to the next.

Timing and speed parameters are not used with every cue, but they are a handy tool that allow for smooth, slow transitions and changing of parameters that might not be crossfadable. It is extremely important that you study your fixture's DMX protocol to determine exactly how these speed functions relate. Each manufacturer has their own methods, and often these can change between fixtures. Then be sure not to crossfade and use speed channels at the same time. Finally, ensure you disable the speed functions when they are not needed. These powerful functions are often misunderstood and underused; however, with a little reading and practice, they can be easily mastered.

PALETTES

Once you have patched the console, created groups, and become familiar with your fixtures, you should begin building position palettes. Depending upon your console, these might be referred to as palettes, presets, memories, etc. These are references used to quickly select common positions used when programming. Most programmers take the time to build positions that they feel will be used within the production. Once the positions are stored in the console, they are available for instantaneous recall, without having to move fixtures manually into position. In addition, if your cues refer to the palette (instead of pan and tilt values), then you can update the palette values and the cues will simultaneously update with the new information. This can be a lifesaver when the director decides to move an acting area upstage by two feet. You simply adjust the fixtures in that position palette and all your cues referencing the palette will be corrected. Position palettes are commonly used in touring productions as the lighting rig rarely hangs at the same height and location relative to the stage. Palettes allow for the updating of only a small number of positions instead of a large number of cues.

First, look at the stage and try to determine common positions for the fixtures. If the show has a band with a singer, guitar player, bass player, and drummer, then these would be obvious positions to build. It is best to focus every fixture in each of these common positions. That way, if the LD asks for fixture #28 in the drummer position, you can quickly select the fixture and the position. Even if you are programming a one-off type show and do not plan on using the updating features of palettes, they will be extremely useful when building cues. By spending a few hours building position palettes, you can save many more hours when programming, as you do not need to move each fixture individually for each cue. The cue building process is made simpler by allowing you to select very quickly the common positions for the fixtures (see Table 4.2).

Table 4.2 Common Position Palettes

Stage Areas	Stage Washes	House Areas	Specials
Downstage Right	50/50	Audience	Podium
Downstage Center	Straight Down	Random Audience	Orchestra
Downstage Left	Downstage Edge	Up and Out	Front of House
Midstage Right	Cyc or Backdrop	Straight Up	Band Postitions
Midstage Center	Stage Wash	Fan Outs	Acting Areas
Midstage Left	Cross Stage Wash	Blinders	
Upstage Right	Random Stage	Venue Walls	
Upstage Center	Floor Wash		
Upstage Left			

In addition, building color and gobo palettes can produce the same benefits. In the same manner as building position palettes, most desks allow for the creation of palettes with any parameter of the fixtures. Imagine having to continuously color mix the same shade of blue for each cue! A color palette allows for instantaneous selection of this color. Then if the LD or director of the show decides the blue is too pale and asks you to change all cues using that color of blue, you simply update the palette and not each and every cue. Once again programming and editing will be accelerated due to the ease of palette selection and modification. For example, if the LD asks for "fixture #19 upstage center in red with the cone gobo," you could achieve this in a few simple keystrokes.

Prior to building palettes, it is a good idea to home (or recalibrate/ reset) your fixtures. If the fixtures are out of calibration when you build your palettes, then the palettes will be misaligned after the fixtures are recalibrated (or even powered on and off), causing you to have to touch up your palettes.

Some other palettes you might want to consider building are iris, frost, intensity, and fixture homing or shutdown. The more palettes you premake, the less time you will spend in cue creation dialing through values. However, do not allow this preparation to get out of hand, as you do not want to spend all your time building palettes and groups.

Quality is often better than quantity, so it is suggested that you only create the groups and palettes that you think will be used with the production. The more palettes you have the more that will need updating in the future. In addition, a large number of palettes can slow down your programming if you have to search through hundreds of palettes to find the desired position or color. A good programmer will discover the perfect amount of palettes for each situation. Some productions will require hundreds of palettes, while others only a few. Your ability to determine the essentials for each production while also maximizing the output potential of the fixtures will aid the LD's overall process in creating a successful production.

5

Intermediate Programming

Once an automated lighting programmer understands the basic concepts of programming consoles and fixtures, the skills beyond console syntax and DMX protocols must be learned. There are specific routines that programmers use daily, yet these skills are rarely detailed in manufacturers' manuals. This chapter discusses these talents and describes why they are important.

MARK CUES

One of the most important elements of good programming is an excellent transition from cue to cue. If a show is programmed with no consideration to how the fixtures change from cue to cue, then the programming can look sloppy. When you notice fixtures moving into place as they fade up or abrupt gobo changes, chances are these are unintended mistakes. The programmer probably did not take the time to preassign the fixtures in their new settings. An essential tool to prevent these mistakes is the mark cue or setup cue. Some consoles either automate this process entirely or have tools to make it easier, while other consoles leave it to the programmers to build their own mark cues. Regardless of your console, it is important to understand how to build mark cues and what they are used for.

The most common example for a mark cue begins with a simple transition of scenes in a theatrical show. If cue five has two fixtures fade out on stage right, then cue six has the same two fixtures fade up on stage left, you will see the need for mark cues. As the fixtures are fading up on stage left, they will also be moving from stage right to left. This is not the desired effect, as you only wanted to see them fade up in their new position. What you need is for the fixtures to move in black (MIB) to their new position. This will require a cue between cues 5 and 6 (5.5) that presets or marks the fixtures. Usually you will assign a time to cue 5.5 so that it will occur automatically once cue 5 is complete. This way when you trigger cue 6, the fixtures will simply fade up already in their new position. Cue 5.5 would now be a mark or setup cue.

Visually the mark cue does nothing, but in reality it is preparing the fixtures for their next cue. As soon as the blackout of the two fixtures finishes (cue 5), the mark cue is played (cue 5.5). It moves the fixtures into their new position while still in black. Then when the fade up cue is played (cue 6), the fixtures are already in position and simply fade up without moving. My example is with positions, but can be applied to any attribute of the fixture. For example, let's say you have a gobo wash on a cyclorama in cue 10, fade out in cue 11, then fade up again with a new gobo wash in cue 12. You will need to place a mark cue at 11.5 to change the gobo while the fixtures are in black. If you do not have a mark cue, then you will see the gobos change while the gobo wash is fading up in cue 12.

Oftentimes the need for a mark cue is not known until the cues are played back. Only then do you notice that fixtures are not preset for their next cue. When you replay your cues in rehearsal and notice fixtures moving into positions while fading up, you should note the cue numbers and create mark cues (unless the move is part of the desired effect). Then the next time your cuelist is played, the mistakes will no longer be a part of the show.

Tricks of the Trade

When building cues you need to think both forward and backward to determine where a fixture is coming from and where it is going. If you are aware of this while building cues your programming will go quickly and cleanly. There will be no need to add mark cues after the first time playing back the cues. In the previous example, when building cue 12 with the new gobo wash, you can simply save a copy of this cue with intensity at zero for cue 11.5. This way you will have created the mark cue at the same time you created the original cue.

Another good trick when building mark cues is to create an intensity palette with all fixtures at an intensity of zero. Next, label this palette "MARK." Now every time you build a mark cue instead of setting the intensity to zero, select this palette for the fixtures you wish to mark. The fixtures will be assigned an intensity of zero, but instead of indicating 0%, the console will display the palette name "MARK" (assuming your desk has these functions). The data in your cue will indicate to you that those fixtures are being marked because the intensity channel will be labeled as such. If your desk allows for tracking, you can then look at the contents of a cue anytime and see that the fixtures are marked. This will save confusion later on when adding cues as you will be able to tell the difference between fixtures that simply have an intensity of zero and those that are marking (although both will actually have an intensity of zero).

Many automated lighting programmers use unique numbering to help identify their mark cues. For instance, cue 20 might be followed by a mark cue at 20.05 and cue 22.2 by 22.25. This method places a 5 at the 100ths place digit of the cue number and allows for quick and easy identification of mark cues. In addition, if the console allows for naming of cues, the cue could be named "mark." The most important factor to remember is to be consistent with your numbering and labeling so that all mark cues (and only mark cues) use the unique scheme.

Once your mark cues are built, you must also consider the timing of the mark. If you are presetting fixtures in a new position with a mark cue, you need to ensure the fixtures are in the new position before it is time for the fade up cue. If the mark cue does not have time to complete, then the fixtures will not be fully marked. On the other hand, some situations require slow marks. For example, if you have moving-head fixtures on the stage, you might not want them moving quickly into their new position as it could be distracting. In this case you might assign a few seconds crossfade to your mark cue so the fixtures move slowly into position (assuming you have enough time between cues). Also, when marking color scrollers, it is important to consider the speed at which the mark happens. If the mark occurs instantly and the scroll runs the entire length possible, it might be noisy. There is nothing worse than hearing a group of scrollers slam to a new color in the middle of a quiet scene.

Automated Mark Cues

Some consoles have powerful features that allow for automated creation of mark cues or move in black settings. These tools are very useful as they will analyze your programming and determine when a fixture changes from an intensity of zero to an intensity above zero. If the console concludes that the fixture is changing attributes (position, color, gobo, etc.) between the two cues, then it will automatically set up or mark the fixture. This allows for very quick, almost lazy, programming as the desk will correct potential problems for you. However, most consoles with automated marks or move in black features do not give you total flexibility or labeling abilities. For example, a mark cue might be inserted between cues 4 and 5, but there might not be data associated with this in the contents view of the console. If you had built your own mark cue (and not used the automated one from the desk) you would have gained this powerful tool. In addition, many of the automated marking functions do not give you complete control of the mark. If you have conventional fixtures with a gel scroller, you might want to mark the scroller change so the color change happens in black. Some desks do not associate the scroller with the dimmer channel and would miss this in their automated marking function.

Mark cues assist in producing clean lighting transitions, while minimizing distractions to the audience. Shows programmed without regard to what occurs between cues appear sloppy and unprofessional. By taking the time to preset your fixtures, or use console functions to assist in the process, you can drastically improve the quality of your lighting programming. However, keep in mind that not all transitions have to be clean. When planned within the cueing, it is often remarkable to see lights change parameters while fading up. This change adds another element of interest to the lighting cue. Ultimately it is up to the designer to decide what type of effect is desired. Until technology allows the fixtures to read our minds and know what we are going to do next, mark cues will be a vital part of automated lighting programming.

BLOCK CUES

Tracking records only the changes you make to each cue and allows previous values to remain unchanged or track into the current cue. There are, of course, times when you want to prevent values from tracking into your new cue, and this is where block cues come in.

A block cue is defined as a cue that contains all parameters for a fix-ture or fixtures. The block cue will not allow any values to track into it from previous cues or cuelists (see Figure 5.1). This is especially impor-tant when you step back and break your show into sections. For example, when programming a dance recital, cues 1–27 are for the first dance num-ber, 28–42 for the second, and 43–82 for the last dance number of Act I. It would be best to make cues 1, 28, and 43 block cues, so that no values could track into each individual dance number. If you do not build a block cue at the start of each section, then you run the risk of data flow prob-lems. For instance, cue 26 changes the wash lights to indigo. The wash lights do not change values again until cue 40 when they change to red (the color values were not recorded into cues 27–39, allowing the color to track). Then during the dress rehearsal, the LD decides to change the color of cue 26 to green. This change is perfect for the end of the first dance routine (cues 26 and 27), but now the green will also track into cues 28–39, drastically changing the look of the second dance routine. Had cue 28 been a block cue with the color value recorded as indigo, then the changes could have been made to the first routine without affecting the following routines.

By strategically placing block cues into your show, subsections of programming can be created. A block cue can provide a "fresh" start where you know no changes earlier on will affect future cues. Even in unstructured shows carefully placed block cues prove helpful. For exam-ple, if you are simply flying through looks on bump buttons for a one-off concert, most of your cues will probably allow certain attributes to track. You might have a button for a color chase, another for strobe, another for

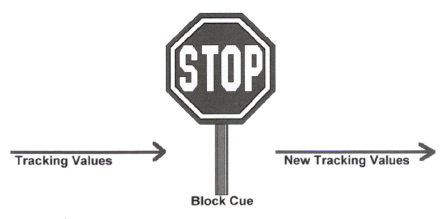

Figure 5.1 A Block Cue Stops the Flow of Tracking Data

ballyhoos, etc. It is good practice to have a look to go to that is fully blocked (maybe at the end of each song). This way when you play the blocked cue, you can be assured that all other chases, effects, etc. will not track into the look. Then from this blocked state, you can continue adding tracking cues to create new looks on stage.

Marking and Blocking

I once programmed an ice skating tour that was running via SMPTE timecode. I had to build the show to prepare for any skater not being able to skate on any given night due to injury, etc. The sound operator would simply skip that portion of the audio track and the associated timecode, causing the lighting console to skip ahead in the cuelist to the beginning of the next number in the show. To prepare the show for these occasions, I had to be sure that my mark cues were also block cues as well as the start of timecode for each skating number. If I had simply allowed the console to jump from one skate number to another without blocking my mark cues, then who knows what kind of wacky looks would have been "created" by skipping portions of the show. Without the block cues in place, the data from the previously played skate routine could have tracked into the next routine. Blocking all values for your marked fixtures ensures that any unwanted tracking information doesn't corrupt your final state on stage.

Organization

When building cues that are also blocked, make a point to note this in the cuelist. If the console has a comments field, I will usually indicate a blocking cue with "BLOCK." This way I can tell at a glance of the cuelist where I have broken the chain of tracking and how I have divided my show. As indicated earlier, usually the mark cue for the beginning of a number of a section of the production will also be the block cue.

Over Blocking

There are, of course, times when blocking can be a hindrance. You would not want to block every single cue in the show, as this would totally eliminate the tracking. If you have a blocking cue in the middle of a dance number and you expected a certain fixture to track its gobo through all the cues, you must make sure the block cue does not destroy the tracking for this fixture. As every show is different, blocking needs will change from production to production. Just as with any tool we have in our programming bag, it is up to you to determine when to block and when to allow values to track. Understanding the value of each option can aid in making any show a success.

EFFECTS GENERATORS

Mathematics is a subject that we all study in school, but generally we allow modern technology to assist us in the more complex algebraic and trigonometric functions of everyday life. Our lighting consoles perform a great deal of math with every function programmed into them and usually we do not even think about how the consoles operate. However, by understanding the basic principles involved, we can better use the applications to achieve our end goal on stage. Most automated lighting consoles now come with some sort of effects generator. Each of these systems might appear different, but underneath they all operate on the same principle: math! That's right. The console's automatic effects are comprised of simple trigonometry formulas such as: $y = a \sin[b \, (x - c)] + d$ and $\sin(x) * \cos(3 * x) * pi/2$.

While Hipparchus (190 B.C.–120 B.C.), known as the father of trigonometry, might have no problem with these formulas, they are not an efficient method of programming automated lighting. Luckily the gurus who write console operating systems do remember their trigonometry and they have created wonderful interfaces for us to use. Everything from premade circles to rainbow chases, to hand-drawn shapes are now as easy as one press of a button. I even know of one console that will allow you to enter your own trigonometric formulas to apply effects (why you would torture yourself in this manner I do not know). In order to create original effects and not just utilize the premade shapes of a console, it is extremely important to understand the underlying principles at work within an effects generator.

The DMX Protocol

The DMX protocol of a fixture is based on a number of control channels, each with 256 values. The value of each channel relates to a specific function of the fixture. Since most fixtures have a dimmer channel where a value of 0 is no output and a value of 255 is full output, I will use this in my examples of effects. If you want to create an effect that dims the fixture up and down, then you will need something that changes the value of the dimmer channel from 0 to 255 and back down to 0. This effect will have to send all values between 0 and 255 so that the dimming is linear and does not appear erratic.

Trigonometry to the Rescue

In order to task the console with automatically fading your fixture, you can assign a sine wave effect to the dimmer channel. I will not bore you with the definition of a sine wave, but I will explain what it means to the average lighting programmer. Most automated lighting consoles have some sort of effects generator and the terminology will be different with each; however, the basic concepts remain the same. A sine wave is a curve that starts from a *base value* and increases and decreases the same amount from that starting point at a specified rate. If you start with a dimmer value of DMX-128 (50%), and have a full sized sine wave, then your fixture will dim up and down at a rate defined by your console (see Figure 5.2).

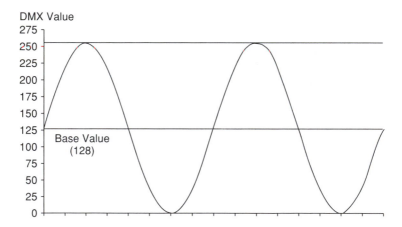

Figure 5.2 An Example of a Sine Wave Effect with a Base Value of 128

Modifying the Starting Point

Because the sine wave is increasing and decreasing the same amount from the starting point, a full sized effect will cause the fixture to dim up and down. If you start with a value of 255 and apply a full sized sine wave, then the values will increase above 255 for half of the sine wave. Because DMX protocol does not allow for anything higher than 255, the dimmer will remain open for half of the effect and only dip to 128 (50%) for the other half (see Figure 5.3).

Modifying the Size and Rate

If you alter the *size* of the sine wave, you can produce an effect that travels through different portions of the DMX protocol. For example, a sine wave with a starting point of 128 (50%) at full size will travel from 0 to 255. However, the same effect with a size of 50% will yield a fade from 64 to 192 (25–75%). In a similar fashion, the *rate* of the effect will adjust the speed at which the fade occurs. By adjusting the effect's rate, you can slow down or speed up the fade. However, it is important to remember that although your console might send the DMX values at an extremely fast rate, your mechanical fixture probably will not be able to keep up. For instance, if you have a sine wave on a dimmer fading from 0 to 255 and you set the rate to 2000 cycles a second, you will probably

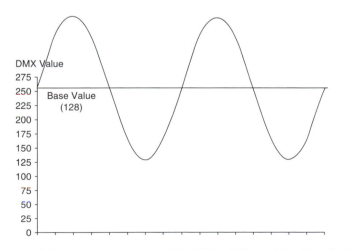

Figure 5.3 An Example of a Sine Wave Effect with a Base Value of 255

only see the fixture increase and decrease slightly from the base value. This is because most mechanical dimmers cannot move this fast. However, many times this will create a totally unexpected result that can be utilized in your programming.

Offsetting Each Fixture

Now you should be able to create an effect where all your fixtures are dimming from 0 to 255. Because all your fixtures have the same effect, size and rate, they will be dimming together. Most consoles allow you to alter the starting point of the effect. For example, by default all your fixtures might be starting at a point in the sine wave equal to DMX-128. However, if you *offset* the point in the curve where each fixture starts, then your effect will be much more dynamic. If you have six fixtures in a row on a truss and you adjust the offset of each slightly more than the previous (the second fixture starts its fade after the first, etc.), then you will have created a linear dimming chase (see Figure 5.4). If you randomly adjust the offset, then the fixtures will be randomly dimming up and down.

Different Wave Forms

Usually your console will offer different types of effects waves or tables to choose from. Some of these include sine, cosine, sawtooth, step, and ramp.

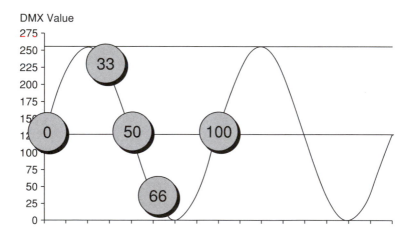

Figure 5.4 An Example of Offset Starting Points within a Sine Wave Effect

Each of the different effects will alter the way the DMX values are changed. For example, a step effect will jump from one value to another without crossfading. A ramp effect will crossfade in one direction and snap in the other. It is a good idea to familiarize yourself with the definition of each effect provided in your console (Figure 5.5).

Other Parameters

Now that you have a basic understanding of how effects operate on the dimmer channel, let's look at a couple more complex situations. Many

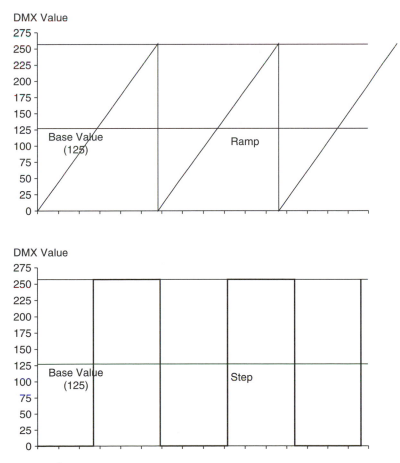

Figure 5.5 Examples of Ramp and Step Wave Effects

hard edge fixtures include an iris, and often the protocol for this channel will include built-in effects (see Table 5.1).

If you wanted to create an effect that opens and closes the iris, then you would need a starting value of 64 and a size of 50 (resulting in a DMX output of 0–128). Otherwise your effect would travel into the portions of the protocol used for iris strobes and ramp snaps. In the same manner, if you want to build an effect that bounces between two gobos, you will need to find an appropriate starting point and size. For instance, the base value of the effect should be equal to a value between the two gobos and not a value equal to either gobo. When building effects, it is a good idea to have the fixture's DMX protocol nearby so you can verify which DMX values to assign to the effect.

Use Them Wisely

Effects generators are wonderful tools for lighting programmers; however, they can also be very annoying when overused or used without understanding. All too often I see people who use these generators for the majority of their programming and usually they have no idea what is going on. For example, if you need to create a ballyhoo on stage and select a premade effect from your console, then you should take the time to adjust the starting value and size so the fixtures only move in the desired locations. By looking at effects as another item in your bag of tricks, then you can effectively utilize them in your show.

FYI: Effects Engine™

A little known lighting industry fact is that Flying Pig Systems registered a trademark on the term "Effects Engine" when they first

Table 5.1 Sample Iris DMX Protocol

DMX Channel	DMX Value	Effect
9 Iris	0–10	Closed
	11–119	Varied Sizes (small to large)
	120–130	Full Open
	131–200	Varied Speed Ramp Snap (includes shutter)
	201–240	Varied Speed Iris Pulse
	241–255	Full Open

introduced it into their lighting console. While this has no bearing on other consoles creating similar functions, it does legally give Flying Pig Systems the exclusive use of this term as it relates to lighting consoles.

KICKIN' IT OLD SCHOOL

I have been programming automated lights for so many years that often I forget the education that occurred in my early years. Just as we learned as programmers what to do with the fixtures and consoles, so did the manufacturers. Many tasks that had to be created by hand are now automatic functions of the fixtures or desks. However, I still apply the concepts I learned in the beginning with every programming session I am involved with. Many of these "classic" programming techniques are lost in a wash of autogenerated effects in modern shows.

Fireworks

Here is the situation: You have 12 hard edge fixtures and a nice backdrop. You want to give the feeling of individual firework shells going off in the distance (see Figure 5.6). One way to achieve this effect would be to have one fixture come on, expand like a firework, and disappear. Then repeat similar looks with the other fixtures one at a time.

A common method of creating this chase would be as follows. You first need to build a look with all twelve fixtures on the backdrop. Place each fixture in a different location and in different colors and/or gobos. As you build this look, remember the image with all fixtures on at the same time will not be seen, only one fixture at a time. So do not worry if some fixtures overlap or contrast with each other. Now that the look is built, you need to preset the fixtures for the chase. Select all twelve fixtures, set the iris to the smallest setting, and close the shutter. Record this as cue one of the chase. Now again select all twelve fixtures, set the iris to the smallest, and close the shutter. Record this as cues 2–12 with a crossfade time of zero. I am assuming your console uses tracking; if not, then record cues 2–12 the same as cue 1 (with all values for all fixtures). Now you should have twelve cues with all fixtures set to small iris and a closed shutter. Of course, on stage this will appear as no output, so obviously there is more work to be done!

Figure 5.6 Fireworks Gobos Used with a Fireworks Chase

Making the Magic

To make the real magic of this cue, you must now edit each of the twelve cues. In the first cue, select fixture one and open the shutter and assign the iris to full. Rerecord these changes to cue one, then begin editing cue two. In cue two select fixture two and open the shutter and set the iris to full. Continue similar edits through all twelve cues. Now when you play the cuelist, or chase, you will see each fixture open its shutter and iris out. Then when the next step of the chase occurs, that fixture will close its shutter and another will open its shutter and iris. You will need to adjust the rate of the chase to match the speed of the iris in your fixtures (usually around 1 second a step).

The great thing about building a chase in this manner is that it has the mark cues built in. As each fixture closes its shutter, it will also reset its iris to the minimum setting. This allows it to be ready to repeat the look the next time the cue comes around. In addition, to make the chase more interesting, you can randomize the order. If your console will play chases in random order, there is no worry about which fixture is setup for the next cue, as they all are always preset. When using a console without a randomize feature, you can create the original cues in a random order. Instead of selecting the fixtures in numeric order while editing cues 1–12, you could select them randomly. I usually write out the numbers 1 through 12 on a piece of paper. Then as I randomly edit each fixture, I put a check mark next to each one that I have used. This way I do not repeat any fixtures and I know when I have used all of them.

Timing

It is important to understand why this chase works with a zero crossfade time. The shutter will open and close instantly, yet the iris will take about 1 second to open. This is due to mechanics of the iris. To change the look on stage to appear as raindrops, you can simply select different gobos and colors and put a crossfade time on the iris. If you slow down the iris (to around 2 seconds) and increase the amount of time on each step, then the cue will appear different. If your chase is running faster than the iris moves, then you will not see the iris fully open. In this case, add more time to remain on each step of the chase longer.

Modern Miracles

This section is entitled "Kickin' It Old School" because in the early days of automated lighting programming, this is how we had to build our chases. Now many consoles and fixtures have built-in effects. Take a look at the DMX protocol for most hard edge fixtures manufactured today and you will find a "ramp snap" or "pulse" setting for the iris. These will close the shutter and iris on the fixtures and then randomly open them one at a time. By using this setting, you no longer have to program a chase to create a fireworks effect. In addition, most automated lighting consoles contain effects generators that can be used to ease in the programming of these looks.

Applying Concepts

Hopefully you can begin to form other ideas from this basic programming concept (e.g., if you need to create a color that sweeps through a series of fixtures). By applying the lessons learned with this simple fireworks chase, you should be able to create a chase that adds in a color mixing parameter one fixture at a time while resetting from the previous step. In addition, this exercise reinforces the practice of building mark cues and repetitive tasks. The next time you find yourself in a situation where you need to make a large chase that resets after each step, think about building all the marks first, then going back and editing in the actual changes. Lighting programmers have many "tricks" at our disposal, but we must look at each situation and decide how to apply them for any given situation. I do not build as many fireworks chases today as I did ten years ago, but I certainly use the methods I learned from it on every show.

COMMON CHASES

The following list describes some common chases that make for great programming exercises. Each one makes use of various programming principles and concepts. A good lighting programmer should be able to build any of the following fairly easily. In addition, the programmer should recognize multiple methods for creating each look, such as using built-in fixture effects or console effects generators.

1. **Kicks**—All fixtures are blacked out and pointing down on the stage. One at a time, a fixture will turn on its intensity and move to a position pointing upward. As it finishes its move, it will blackout and return to its starting position while at the same time another fixture will begin a similar move.
2. **Ballyhoo**—All fixtures move about in an area (stage or audience) in a random type fashion.
3. **Stabs**—All fixtures are irised down to their smallest size and placed in a static position with no intensity. Then one fixture at a time snaps to full intensity. As each fixture snaps on, the previous fixture snaps off. Oftentimes, stabs are built using multiple positions with the fixtures changing positions when blacked out.
4. **Fading Pulse**—All fixtures randomly fade intensity from 0–100%.
5. **Indigo/Red**—A rapid snap change from an indigo or congo color to a red or orange color. Usually all fixtures change at the same time.
6. **Random Strobe**—All fixtures strobe at various rates to create a random strobing effect.
7. **Fireworks/Droplets**—Fireworks as described earlier snaps the intensity to full and irises out fixtures one at a time in a random order.

Table 5.2 Rainbow Color Chase

Step 1	100% cyan,	0% magenta,	0% yellow
Step 2	100% cyan,	100% magenta,	0% yellow
Step 3	0% cyan,	100% magenta,	0% yellow
Step 4	0% cyan,	100% magenta,	100% yellow
Step 5	0% cyan,	0% magenta,	100% yellow
Step 6	100% cyan,	0% magenta,	100% yellow

Droplets is very similar; however, it snaps the intensity to full and irises *in* fixtures one at a time in a random order.

8. **Line Chase**—All fixtures are blacked out, then turn on one at a time in a linear order. Usually this chase is used with fixtures placed all in a row.

9. **Smooth Color Mix (Rainbow)**—Color mixing fixtures crossfade through all possible colors except white. They are often created with six steps or cues as shown in Table 5.2.

10. **Gobo Rockers**—Rotating gobos are set to an indexed position and then crossfaded or snapped between two indexed positions. This causes the gobo to rock back and forth.

There are many variations on these chases as well as multiple names and descriptions. Over time you should learn to recognize common programming principles and develop many that are unique to your style of programming.

6

Advanced Programming

The many facets of automated lighting programming allow for different levels of programmers. Very accomplished programmers may never utilize show control or visualization, while others will depend upon them during nearly every production. Budgetary and time constraints often dictate the use of advanced programming functionalities, while others will use these concepts to further the capabilities of the lighting. It is important for an automated lighting programmer to be aware of the advanced programming techniques that he or she might encounter.

VISUALIZATION

Many years ago I attended a lighting seminar in New York. While there, I met another student who told me about a new product about to be introduced at the upcoming Lighting Dimensions International (LDI) tradeshow. He said some friends in Canada had developed software that allowed them to program their moving lights by looking at a representation of them on a computer screen. This software would allow them to preprogram in a virtual world and then later plug in the real fixtures. They hoped their new idea would start a revolution in the automated lighting world. This software quickly grew into the industry standard visualization tool we know today as WYSIWYG (what you see is what you get).

There are now several different brands of lighting visualization software, and even some lighting consoles with built-in or proprietary software. All of these programs serve one basic purpose, to allow you to see the final result of your programming data without attaching genuine fixtures.

How It Works

Visualization software in its most basic form is a virtual lighting rig that you program using any standard DMX console. The software does little more than emulate what a real lighting rig would do, thereby allowing programmers to use their console to create or edit a show without an actual lighting rig. All programming data and cueing remains in the lighting console making the transition to a real lighting rig very simple (just plug in the DMX). Early versions of the software were simple wire-frame drawings of the fixture's output, but now sophisticated rendering systems and even 3D environments are commonplace. Visualization software can do many things to aid a designer and others involved with a production; however, for the purpose of this book I will try to focus on the programming aspects alone.

Benefits

One of the biggest reasons to use visualization software is the substantial savings involved. If you can spend half of your programming time in the virtual world, then the production will save thousands of dollars. The cost to rent a venue, hire a crew, rent equipment, etc. is usually much higher than the use of a console, computer, and software. This means that quite often your programming time can increase, allowing more flexibility and creativity in your work. In addition, the FOH area can be anywhere you like. You can work in a comfortable environment at any hours you and the LD desire.

Building cues while staring at a computer screen also has other advantages. I usually find the programming time with visualization a great period to "learn" the rig, the LD's intentions, and the production details. If you discover that the downstage truss fixtures will not reach all the needed locations, you can easily move them to a new position without calling in the crew. In addition, this period is often used to setup everything in the console prior to programming (palettes, groups, colors, SMPTE timecode, etc.).

Programming

Programming with a visualizer is no different than programming with an actual lighting rig. All the functions of your console are still available to you. However, there are many things you must consider when working in a virtual world. Most of the visualization programs work very hard to reproduce exactly how real fixtures output, but there are often differences. In the virtual world things often move at different speeds than in the real world. You might find that your fixtures can move from stage right to stage left in half a second on the computer screen, but the actual fixtures are not able to move as quickly. When programming with a visualizer, it is very important to understand that you will probably need to touch up your cues. In addition, most modern fixtures have automated functions such as strobing or gobo wheel rotations. Often these speeds will also be different on screen than with a real fixture. That perfect strobe setting that flashed with the musical beat during preprogramming might turn out to be twice as fast with the actual rig. It is a good idea to have one of each fixture in your rig hooked up live while working with a visualizer. This way you can check the colors, speeds, etc. on that one fixture and learn how it differs from the computerized version.

Most automated lighting consoles make use of palettes (also known as position memories, presets, focus points, etc.). These are references to specific values that can be recorded into cues. If you change the value of the reference, all your cues using it will also update. Palettes become extremely important when programming with a visualizer. There are too many real world factors to enable you to take a show programmed virtually and run a perfect show without updating any information. For example, a slight deviation in the angle of the fixtures can cause them to project in the wrong positions. The most important thing to remember when working with a visualizer is that it can only simulate the real world and you will need to make changes accordingly.

Cueing

The ability to structure your show is one of the most valuable benefits of working with a visualizer. Frequently rough cue ideas are created virtually and later made complete with the real fixtures. The rough cue data, however, will act as a placeholder of the LD's concepts, and, more importantly, the timing of the show. Expect to make changes to the look of a cue simply because it appears much different in reality versus the computer screen. Also when working with timecode, visualizers provide a superb opportunity to enter cue times and perfect the cueing construction.

Two-Way Communication

Most visualizer software packages have a method of communicating with supported consoles. This allows an LD to create his drawings and paperwork within the software and then send the patch information to the lighting console. In addition, oftentimes you can use the computer mouse to point to a location on the virtual set. Not only will the fixtures point to this location, but the pan and tilt information will also appear in your console for recording to cues or palettes. We are just now beginning to see the "Holy Grail" of lighting visualization: blind or preview capabilities. This function allows programmers to build or preview information on the visualization software without outputting DMX to the lighting rig. During a show, the programmer can modify an upcoming cue while looking at a representation of it.

Program Anywhere

Thanks to a group of Canadians emulating real fixtures, the automated lighting industry was revolutionized. There are many visualization studios around the world where an LD and programmer can simply walk in and begin working. In addition to reducing costs and aiding in cue creation, visualizers are a great learning tool. Students can now learn the functions of a console and fixtures with much less expense. Many console offline editors work directly with a visualizer, eliminating the need for a console. I enjoy programming real fixtures as much as I enjoy playing "lighting video games" with a visualizer. Imagine sitting on a plane, preprogramming your show as if you were sitting in a venue with a full lighting rig. Trust me, it is a lot of fun (especially during turbulence)!

IT'S TIME FOR TIMECODE

Many productions require the lighting to be perfectly synchronized with the audio or video elements. While this can be achieved manually with a good operator, the best method is to use some sort of show control to automate the lighting cues. One of the more common approaches is to use a form of timecode.

The History of Timecode

In the days of film (before videotape), audio synchronization was achieved mechanically. The film itself and audiotapes had sprocket holes that would allow for perfect synchronization of the two sources. When videotape was developed without sprockets, an electronic method for synchronizing was created. In 1967 the Society of Motion Picture and Television Engineers developed SMPTE timecode. This standard was based upon an eight-digit twenty-four-hour clock.

In addition to SMPTE, there are several other types of timecode including MIDI timecode (MTC). MTC is very similar to the SMPTE timecode, but in a different protocol. Depending on your production and your lighting console, you might talk about SMPTE but actually use MTC. Throughout this book when timecode is mentioned, it can be any of the actual forms.

Defining Timecode

The first two digits represent the hour (0–23), the next two the minute (0–59), then the second (0–59), and finally the frame (0–xx). Notice I did not give a range for the frames. The frame rate will change depending upon the standard used. Currently there are four typical frame rate standards, each with a different value of frames per second or fps (see Table 6.1).

Table 6.1 Common Frame Rate Standards

NAME	*FPS*
SMPTE 30	30
NTSC 30 or SMPTE 30 drop frame	29.97
EBU	25
FILM	24

SMPTE 30 is the original SMPTE standard often used in the audio industry. NTSC 30 or SMPTE 30 drop frame is mostly used by the NTSC video industry. This frame rate is based on 30fps, but two frame counts are dropped at the start of every minute, except for every tenth minute. EBU is commonly used in Europe by the PAL video industry, and FILM, as the name implies, is used by the film industry.

I do not want to scare you by going into in-depth explanations of how timecode functions in the binary and linear worlds. However, there are many books and websites dedicated to the subject if you are interested in learning more.

Timecode and Lighting

Imagine building a very complex lighting show that executes 1200 cues in 3 minutes. These cues coincide with specific music notes of the audio track. At the very moment the short production is concluded, the show repeats again with the same perfection. This type of accuracy would be near impossible for a human operator to obtain, so another form of synchronized triggering is needed. Synchronizing your lighting to an audio or video track is a very simple process involving timecode.

The first step is to decide that you need to use timecode to trigger your lighting. Make sure your production has elements that will generate the timecode. For example, if you are working on a live play, you probably will not have a recorded source that the actors synchronize to. If you are working on an dance show where each number runs from a digital audiotape (DAT), then you have a sync source. You will need to work with the audio crew to ensure they provide you with the type of timecode required for your console.

Now that you have the timecode source confirmed, you can build your lighting cues as you normally would. After the cues are in the console, you can go back and assign a trigger time to each. Many consoles allow you to "teach" the trigger times to the cuelist. When using a "learn timing" method, you will playback your audio or timecode source and then simply press your console's GO button at the appropriate moment in the music. The console will then insert the timecode value for that moment into the trigger time for the cue. Later, when you replay your timecode source, the cues will playback at the exact time locations when you pressed the GO button. You have essentially recorded the timing of your GO presses into the console. I suggest reading your console's manual to determine exactly how to get the timecode times into your cuelist.

Changing Time

Table 6.2 represents a cuelist with timecode trigger points for five cues. By looking at the differences in the numbers, you can gain a lot of information. For example, the last cue happens 2 minutes 41 seconds and 3 frames after the first cue. You can also see there is a little less than 5 seconds between cues 2 and 3. Much information can be gathered by looking at the cue triggering times.

Let's say you replay your cuelist and the lighting for cue 4 is not synchronized with the explosion sound on the audio track. You will first need to determine if the lighting cue occurs too early or too late and then modify the trigger time. Determining how much time to edit can be difficult, but here is a rough guide. Do not begin by editing single frames (unless the cue is just really close). Think of the frames in easier editing blocks. For instance, when using 30fps remember that 15 frames is half a second and 7 frames is about a fourth of a second. I generally begin by editing within half a second and then move to smaller increments.

Hidden Dangers

Right now you might be thinking that working with timecode is a much simpler process than you first thought. You are correct; however, there are some dangers to lookout for. First, you need to make sure that your timecode source does not change once you begin adding timing to your cues. If the times that reference specific points in the audio track are suddenly off by 1 minute 13 frames, then you will have to edit all

Table 6.2   An Example of a Cuelist Using Timecode

01:00:01.21	cue 1
01:00:05.02	cue 2
01:00:10.00	cue 3
01:02:42.22	cue 4
01:02:42.24	cue 5

the times in your cuelist. I have seen many cases where the audio crew will rerecord the tracks and change the timecode values, or maybe they discover they are sending the wrong format and change their settings. When these things happen, you can spend hours editing cue trigger times.

Another element you must consider when using timecode is that there is now an input to your lighting console. If your show begins and you forget to turn on the timecode, then the audio will begin, but the lighting will not. On the other hand, if you leave your timecode input on while you are editing cues and the sound guy decides to press play on the DAT, then your console might jump to an unexpected cue. You need to take care to minimize timecode problems.

Back to the Future

Luckily working with timecode and lighting is usually a very simple process. Many programmers become nervous and concerned the first time they hear the show needs to be triggered via timecode. However, as you can see, there is not that much involved. I will warn you, though, that often LDs love to use timecode because they know that cues can be triggered with every single audio note, and you will find yourself building longer cuelists. I see this as a good thing, as it just means more programming time at the lighting console.

THE MAGIC OF MIDI

There comes a time in every automated lighting programmer's career that they will be asked to use MIDI or MIDI Show Control. MIDI is an acronym for Musical Instrument Digital Interface. It was developed in the early 1980s as a standard method for electronic musical equipment to pass messages to each other. In the early 1990s, many manufacturers of professional entertainment equipment created a special subset of MIDI with unique commands relating to entertainment productions. This new protocol was referred to as MIDI Show Control (MSC). Many automated lighting consoles implemented MIDI and/or MSC to allow remote triggering of lighting consoles and other devices. The following is a broad overview of MIDI and MSC uses as related to automated lighting programming. Many existing books and Internet resources further explain MIDI and MIDI Show Control in-depth.

Lighting Applications

Generally an automated lighting programmer will not need to be an expert with MIDI and MSC. However, there are four basic uses associated with lighting programming that you must be aware of. The first two relate to console redundancy. Many designers insist on a backup lighting console in the event of a failure. Consoles connected via MIDI or MSC often have the capability of real-time playback tracking or complete redundancy. With real-time playback tracking, the main console will send MIDI or MSC commands to the second console ensuring that both consoles are in the same state of playback. Any new programming information will exist only on the main console. On the other hand, complete redundancy uses MIDI or MSC to send every keystroke from the main console to the secondary console. In this scenario, both consoles will always maintain the same state as they are performing identical key presses.

The next two uses of MIDI or MSC commonly used by automated lighting programmers are for interaction with other devices within the production. For example, the automated lighting console might send playback commands to a conventional lighting console. In addition, a lighting console might use MIDI or MSC to trigger a wide assortment of devices such as audio, video, automation, scenic elements, etc. In the same manner, MIDI and MSC can be used for triggering an automated lighting console from show control computers or other devices.

MIDI Notes

MIDI in its simplest form is a networking protocol that allows multiple devices to communicate with simple commands. The command set includes note-ons, note-offs, key velocity, pitch bend, and other methods designed for controlling a synthesizer (see Table 6.3). Sometimes basic MIDI is referred to as "MIDI Notes" due to its musical structure.

To aid with large configurations of equipment, MIDI specifies 16 discrete MIDI Channels. This enables a single cable arrangement to control

Table 6.3 Basic MIDI Commands

NOTE ON	NOTE OFF	Poly Key Pressure	Control Change	Program Change	Mono Key Pressure	Pitch Bend	System

up to 16 different devices at once. The model of MIDI Channels is similar to the concept of a DMX address. Each device is assigned a MIDI Channel number and will listen only to commands sent to that channel. In this manner many devices can be connected in series, yet only respond to commands specific to each device. For example, a show control computer might send commands to an automated lighting console, a conventional lighting console, and an audio desk. All devices will receive the same data from the show control computer, but respond only to their unique commands as defined by the MIDI Channel. When setting up your console to respond to MIDI information, you will need to assign a MIDI Channel number to the console. If your console will be used to transmit MIDI information to trigger other devices, then the output MIDI Channel will need to be defined with each command. Refer to your console's documentation for further details on defining MIDI Channels.

MIDI Show Control

As the use of MIDI grew in the 1980s, many entertainment professionals saw the need for a specialized subset of MIDI. They developed a new standard known as MIDI Show Control. The command set includes load, go, stop, cue number, cuelist number, fire macro, etc. In addition, specific subcommands were developed for industry-based command structures. Each command format of MSC consists of its own types of commands related to the industry type. Some of these industries include: lighting, audio, pyrotechnics, and video (see Table 6.4).

In a similar method to MIDI Channels, MSC defines a Device ID for each unique device. Again, this setting allows each device to receive all MSC commands but only respond to those intended for its unique Device ID. When setting up your console to respond to MSC information you will need to assign an MSC Device ID to the console. If your console will be used to transmit MSC information to trigger other devices, then the output MSC Device ID will need to be defined with each command. Refer to your console's documentation for further details on defining MSC Device IDs.

MSC transmits both commands and command data (see Table 6.5). For instance, an MSC message might send the equivalent of "Device ID 2 Lighting General Format Go Cue 2 Cuelist 7." If a device sends this information to your console, it should trigger the second cue of the seventh cuelist. Unfortunately, many console manufacturers have chosen not to fully implement MSC. Your console might ignore the cuelist number

Table 6.4 MIDI Show Control Command Formats

01 Lighting (General Category)	10 Sound (General Category)	20 Machinery (General Category)	30 Video (General Category)	40 Projection (General Category)	50 Process Control (General Category)	60 Pyro (General Category)
02 Moving Lights	11 Music	21 Rigging	31 Videotape Machines	41 Film Projectors	51 Hydraulic Oil	61 Fireworks
03 Color Changers	12 CD Players	22 Flys	32 Videocassette Machines	42 Slide Projectors	52 H_2O	62 Explosions
04 Strobes	13 EPROM Playback	23 Lifts	33 Video Disc Players	43 Video Projectors	53 CO_2	63 Flame
05 Lasers	14 Audio Tape Machines	24 Turntables	34 Video Switchers	44 Dissolvers	54 Compressed Air	64 Smoke Pots

(continued)

Table 6.4 *(continued)*

06 Chasers	15 Intercoms	25 Trusses	35 Video Effects	45 Shutter Controls	55 Natural Gas		
	16 Amplifiers	26 Robots	36 Video Character Generators		56 Fog		
	17 Audio Effects Devices	27 Animation	37 Video Still Stores		57 Smoke		
	18 Equalizers	28 Floats	38 Video Monitors		58 Cracked Haze		
		29 Breakaways					
		2A Barges					

Table 6.5 Basic MIDI Show Control Commands

Reserved	Go	Stop	Resume	Timed Go	Load	Set	Fire
All Off	Go/Jam Clock	Standby +	Standby –	Sequence +	Sequence –	Start Clock	Stop Clock
Zero Clock	Set Clock	MTC Chase On	MTC Chase OFF	Open Cuelist	Close Cuelist	Open Cue Path	Close Cue Path

portion of the command and instead apply the message to the currently active cuelist (or even to all cuelists). It is extremely important that you read and understand the console's MSC implementation. With a properly configured console, MSC receiving functionality should be relatively simple.

In addition to receiving MSC commands, many lighting consoles also have the ability to transmit MSC messages. Depending upon the functionality of your console, this message might be editable. However, many consoles simply implement MSC to send commands mimicking console activities. For example, if you press GO for cue 2 of cuelist 7, the console will send this information out to a predefined Device ID. Other lighting consoles have methods to send unique MSC commands in the same manner as lighting cues. This ability allows the lighting console to behave as a show control computer by triggering various devices through the use of MSC. Quite often a substantial understanding of MSC (hex codes, commands, formats, etc.) is required. Very few console manufacturers have spent the time to create a user-friendly user interface. Luckily there are many books and Internet resources available regarding MIDI and MSC.

Be Prepared

Unfortunately, most lighting consoles have adopted a rather poor implementation of MIDI and MSC, thus requiring programmers to be familiar with hex codes and other technical jargon. Since MIDI and MSC are rarely used beyond simple triggering or redundant control, manufacturers of lighting consoles have not put much effort into creating user-friendly interfaces. It is essential that a lighting programmer study the user manual of the console to determine exactly how MIDI and MSC function within the console. Fortunately, however, MIDI and MSC use rarely appears as a last minute surprise, thus allowing programmers an opportunity to analyze their console's implementation.

7

Programming Genres

Automated lighting programming can be applied to many different types of productions. From theatre to concerts to permanent installations, the variety of genres available is practically endless. One of the greatest joys for an automated lighting programmer is knowing that every production is different. Just as each production presents unique challenges, there are exclusive programming concepts and techniques applied to each. Many of these ideas can crossover between production types, thus making all equally important to an automated lighting programmer, no matter the production type he or she is involved with.

STRUCTURED AND CORPORATE THEATRE

The very roots of any live performance lie in the theatre. Since before early Roman periods, man has been performing in various venues. The popular theatre, as we know it today, evolved over thousands of years with various lighting methods. Modern theatrical productions often incorporate automated lighting technology into the lighting design. In addition, many corporate events (business meetings, sales promotions, etc.) follow a similar theatrical structure. Automated lighting programming for the theatre requires special procedures to ensure a highly repeatable production (Figure 7.1).

Figure 7.1 Structured and Corporate Theatre Productions Have Unique Requirements

Organization

The very nature of a play or musical requires a structured list of lighting cues. Because there are usually many performances, every element of the show requires perfectly repeatable execution. Usually the rehearsal and preproduction periods for theatrical productions are much longer than other types of productions. During this time all departments involved will perfect and hone their contributions to the production. For the automated lighting programmer, this can be a very tedious time. A scene may have only one establishing lighting cue, then after forty minutes of acting, a blackout at the end. The scene might be rehearsed for days on end without making any changes to the lighting look. The programmer must endure the rehearsal process, yet be ready to make any changes as soon as needed.

The cue to cue organization requires the programmer to maintain order while also ensuring efficient playback. Mark and block cues are essential to an automated lighting programmer working on a theatrical production. Good organizational skills and descriptive labeling of cues, palettes, etc. aid the programmer's effectiveness. At any given moment the LD might request "a washlight pointing stage right in deep blue." The programmer must be aware of fixtures currently in use and/or preparing for use (marked). Only then can the programmer make an educated decision as to which fixture to add to the cue. Once adding the fixture to the current cue, the programmer may need to look back and mark the fixture prior to its use. In addition, the fixture will need to be added to any blackout cue for the scene. Usually the LD will simply make the request to add the fixture to the cue and it will then be up to the programmer to automatically build the mark, block, and blackout cues. A good programmer will accomplish these tasks without the LD ever needing to make a request to do so.

Conventionals

Theatrical lighting usually includes both conventional and automated programming. Some productions will use a specific console for each type of lighting while others will control all lighting from one console. If both conventional and automated lighting will be programmed on one desk, then the automated lighting programmer needs to prepare for conventional programming. Quite often an LD will spend great lengths of time adjusting the intensity values for conventional lights. The programmer should be prepared to adjust levels quickly and easily. Groups, palettes, and quick intensity functions become essential tools for the programmer. Many designers also find it useful for the programmer to repeat tasks to them as they happen. This way the LD can keep their eyes on the stage looking for the level changes. For instance, when asked to bring a conventional channel down 10%, a good programmer will do so quickly and respond by stating the new value. For example, he or she might say "at 60." Then the LD will have a reference to the value and can make another requested change if needed. With the next change the programmer will again state the new value ("at 50"). While this small function can be very helpful to many LDs, it can also be an annoyance to others. Be sure to consult with your LD prior to calling out all level changes. After programming several productions, many programmers find repeating intensity level changes, color or position palette names, and other functions to the LD become habit. Luckily, many designers appreciate this automatic feedback given to them by their programmer.

Dual Consoles

When adding automated lights to a theatrical production, numerous designers choose to have a desk for each type of lighting (conventional and automated). This allows for multitasking as both programmers can be working on different elements of the same cue simultaneously. In this scenario both programmers must ensure they use the same cue numbers and structure. For example, "lighting cue 28" should reference the same point in the show on both consoles. If the conventional desk has a cue 30 and there is no need for a cue on the automated desk, a blank cue should be inserted to maintain uniformity between the two consoles. This will guarantee a consistent cue structure for the production. The LD or stage manager will then be able to call "go cue 30" and both console operators can trigger a cue (without having to check for its existence first).

Some productions will require two different consoles for programming and then utilize only one operator for playback. With two consoles in use during programming, cue creation occurs much faster. The conventional programmer can slowly adjust levels with an LD, while the automated lighting programmer is busy building a complex chase for the same cue. Once the show is programmed and rehearsals are complete, two console operators may not be desired. There are several choices to combine the playback capabilities, allowing one person operation. The first is to have one console trigger the other via MIDI or MIDI Show Control (or other triggering methods). The operator will then simply playback cues from one desk, which will in turn send matching triggering information to the second desk. If both desks are programmed with an identical cueing configuration, then all cues should remain perfectly synchronized.

Another method for reducing the number of consoles required for playback is to capture the data from the conventional console into the automated lighting console. Many sophisticated lighting consoles have the ability to capture and record DMX values. After both consoles are fully programmed, the DMX values output by the conventional desk will be recorded into the automated lighting console on a cue by cue basis. Only DMX values are recorded, so the automated lighting programmer will have to reprogram any timing information. Once all the cues are captured and recorded into the automated lighting console, all playback and future editing will take place from this desk.

Prepared Theatrics

Automated lighting programming for theatrical productions is as fulfilling and challenging as any other genre of lighting. Many times fixtures are used simply as repositionable lighting fixtures and the audience may never realize the automation features. Other production will make full use of obvious fixture movements and output changes. Regardless of the uses, the most common element of theatrical type productions is a structured cueing method.

CONCERT TOURS

Concert tours are a driving force of the automated lighting industry. Almost every musical concert of any genre employs the use of automated lights to enhance the production and save time. There are many techniques used when programming concert tours that are unique to this type of production. An automated lighting programmer must be aware of these requirements when programming for any concert tour (Figure 7.2).

It Is All About the Music

The very first thing you must do, as a programmer of a musical concert, is to listen to the music. Then listen to it again. Keep listening to it until

Figure 7.2 Concert Tour Programming Can Be Very Challenging

every beat, every change, and every nuance (no matter how subtle) is ingrained in your mind. With a good understanding of the music, you will be prepared to understand the goals and desires of the LD. Usually the LD will have discussed his concepts with the artist(s) prior to your programming session. Listen to the LD's ideas and then try to apply them to the music. You must always remember that in most cases the concert is about the music and not a light show. The lighting is there to enhance the overall production, not to override it. After all, the crowd paid money to hear the artist, not watch your lighting programming.

Before You Program

The first thing you need to consider when preparing to program for a concert is who will be operating the console. Sometimes you will not only program the show, but you will also tour with it, operating the desk at every performance. However, if you are hired to simply program the desk and leave it for the LD or another person to take on the road, then there are many special considerations you must make.

When programming a show for another person to operate, you must be very conscious of your organization and labeling. If you label all the cues with strange acronyms that only you understand, how will someone else be able to take over for playback?

Prior to actual building of cues for your concert, you will need to setup palettes (sometimes called presets or memories) in the desk. These are references to quickly select common positions, colors, etc. to be used when programming. In addition, if your cues refer to the palette instead of actual values, then you can update the palette values and the cues will simultaneously update with the new parameter information. Touring shows survive on position palettes. Each day the lighting rig may not be hung in the exact same position, height, and offset from the stage. The operator of the desk must spend a good portion of the preperformance time refocusing each light to the correct position for that day's configuration. For example, if the front truss is one foot higher and two feet further offstage than in the rehearsal space, then all the positions the fixtures point to will be incorrect. However, by simply updating all the position palettes with the correct values for the new configuration, the cues will playback as they were programmed.

When setting up your position palettes, you do not want to make hundreds of positions. Doing so will only result in more work on-site each day. Most concert tours arrive at a venue early in the morning and build the lighting rig and stage. By the time everything is operational, it is usually midafternoon. The operator may have only a few hours to refocus all the fixtures' position palettes. Care must be taken during programming to minimize the number of palettes, while allowing for a multitude of looks throughout the show. As you are programming the show, you must always take into consideration the daily setup time of a tour.

Cue Building

When you and the LD sit down to begin programming the first song, you will probably listen to several versions of the song. Oftentimes musicians play music differently live than on their CD. If you program to a studio mixed CD and time your chases and transitions to match the tempo, don't be surprised when the live version is different.

Just as each musician is different, so are LDs. Sometimes you will build a very structured show with a cuelist (sequence or stack) for each song. Other LDs prefer to have a layout of buttons and faders, where they can "create" lighting looks as the band plays. Depending on the type of music and the LD's preferences, you will often program concert tours in different ways. As stated earlier, it is important to know whom the operator will be and set up the console accordingly. Remember, there are no rules and anything goes.

Standard Operating Procedure

Of course, there is no one method for programming a concert tour; however, there are some common procedures that are often used. Generally an artist will change the set list on various nights of the tour. The band does not always want to play the same songs. Hopefully, you have programmed cues for all the songs you think they will ever play. Then when you are informed each night of the songs to be played, you can simply reorganize your show to accommodate that evening's selection. The order of the songs each night is usually called a "set-list." The set-list will have the song names and breaks or encores listed. This does not mean the band will actually follow the list, but it gives you an idea of what they plan to play at that performance.

Most automated lighting consoles have a function known as pages. Each page will contain a certain number of playbacks with specific cues loaded into buttons on the console. Programmers will organize a concert by using one page per song. For example, page one might be for "Silent Night" and page two for "Deck the Halls." If the artist has 28 songs in their repertoire, then you will need to have a page for each song. On each page, you will have cues, presets, chases, etc. that you created specifically for that song. As the band changes from one song to the next, you simply change the page on the console to prepare for each new song. The console will usually have a method to reorder the pages so you can match the set-list for each performance. In this way you can quickly organize the programming in the desk to match the artist's decision for the set-list.

Every Concert Is Different

There are no hard fast rules about programming automated lights for concert tours. The great fun is that they are all different. Due to requirements of the show, the LD, and the artist(s), every tour is completely different. There is no magic formula for creating the perfectly programmed show, but with some consistency you can make the process simple.

TELEVISION EVENTS

Many television productions utilize automated lighting to create bold movements or color chases. Other programs simply use the technology as remotely, refocusable lighting sources. Award shows, game shows, and musical variety acts commonly benefit from an automated lighting rig. In each of these situations, the lighting designer must make special considerations for the cameras. When working as a lighting programmer for television events, it is essential that these unique requirements are taken into consideration with every button press on the console (Figure 7.3).

The Cameras Are Your Eyes

The significance of the camera's point of view to the lighting programmer cannot be overstated. The most important thing to remember when programming for a television show is that the picture on the screen is the ultimate purpose of the show. You must not lose sight of this goal when helping to create perfect television pictures. One of the most common questions about television lighting is: "Do you worry about how it

Figure 7.3 Televised Events Add a New Eye to the Situation

appears to the live audience?" Generally the answer is no, because the live audience for a television event basically becomes another element of the set. Again, the goal is to create a television show for all the (potentially) millions of viewers, and not a live event for the local audience. Everything *must* be considered based on how it looks on television. This can create some problems for the programmer, but can also open up some unique possibilities.

In order to know exactly how the event will look on screen, the programmer will require a program monitor. A program monitor will allow him to see exactly what the viewing audience will see (called the line cut). In addition, the programmer commonly will have a second monitor with a video switcher. The switcher will allow the programmer to view any of the camera shots at any time (regardless of what is on the line cut). By selecting between the camera shots, the lighting programmer will be able to check each shot before the video director changes to one on the line cut. When building positions, colors, cues, etc. the programmer needs to watch the monitors to determine how the lighting appears on camera. For instance, all the upstage lights fanned out to the audience position may look great from FOH, but then not even show on camera. If the cameras don't shoot it, then it does not exist. Generally when sitting at FOH programming for a television event, programmers spend 90% of their time looking at their television monitors. Many programmers become so focused on the screen that they forget they are actually sitting at the event they are watching on their monitors.

Adjusting for the Camera

Television cameras respond to lighting much differently than the human eye. Intensity levels, colors, angles, etc. all need to be considered from the camera's point of view. The human eye is very forgiving when it comes to different lighting intensities; it has an amazing ability to balance high and low light levels. Unfortunately, television cameras do not have the same abilities. The LD will want to balance all levels so the overall on-screen picture is correct. I will not get into the design aspect here as I am writing about programming, but it is important to understand some television lighting basics. The more you can understand the designer's intended picture quality, the better you can help create the overall look of the show in a quick and efficient manner. By watching the monitors at all times you can determine what lighting elements are in the camera shots and how the lighting will affect them. For example, if you have a nice gobo wash on the backdrop it might look great in the wide shot. However, when the video director cuts to a close up, the background of the image might overpower the followspot intensity on the performer. You may find that setting the intensity of the gobo wash to 50% will work well in both the wide and close-up shots. By anticipating these types of things, the initial programming will require much less adjustment when viewed on camera.

The lighting designer will be concerned with the aesthetic appearance of the background of the camera shots. The programmer must also take this into consideration when building looks. Again imagine a gobo wash on the backdrop. In the wide shot it might appear as the best gobo wash that was ever created, but in the close-up shot there is nothing visible in the background. You might have to move some fixture positions around to ensure the background of the close-up is perfect (without destroying the look of the overall wash). When lighting set pieces, care should be taken not to waste time lighting pieces that will never be shown (or lighting them from the wrong angle). Television crews have some amazing technology in their bag of tricks. They often use jibs (a camera mounted on a crane) and Steadicams (a camera mounted to a human). These types of cameras will shoot from angles you never thought of. By paying attention to what the video director decides to shoot in rehearsal, you can determine what needs to be lit.

Colors and Their Temperature

Television cameras must be balanced to a specific color temperature. This setting will determine exactly how colored lighting will appear on camera. Most automated lighting fixtures use lamps with a high color temperature around 6500°K. Usually, but not always, television shows are balanced to a low color temperature around 3200°K. This will result in colored lights appearing different on camera than to the eye. An open white fixture will be blue on camera. In addition, all other colors will have a bluish tint. Pure magenta takes on a purple color when viewed on screen. Understanding these differences and taking them into account when building palettes and cues is essential for good television lighting. Also, you must be constantly thinking in terms of the television colors and not the eye colors. For example, if the LD asks for a pale lavender wash, you would actually bring a light pink color into the fixtures (on camera, however, it will look lavender). Over time you should be able to predict how certain colors will appear on camera and build palettes and cues before your monitors arrive.

The Magic of Television

As I have stated, you must consider what the camera sees when programming automated lighting for television productions. Because the camera's view is the main perspective for everything you do, this can present new advantages versus programming for the live audience. Remember, if the camera does not see it, then it does not exist. You can actually use this unique television feature to your benefit. For example, I was programming a televised ice skating competition and did not know the order of the skaters' routines. I had built cues for each, but did not have clean transitions from one skater's end look to the next one's beginning cue. At the end of each routine, the video director would cut from a shot of the ice to a close up of the skater receiving their score. As soon as I saw this change on my line-cut monitor, I would change the lighting look on the ice. Then after the skater received his marks, the video director changed the shot back to a nice new look on the ice. The cameras did not pick up the "messy" transition from one ice look to another, although the live audience did see it. Often during awards shows the stage lighting will change while the cameras are on the presenters.

The Magic Box

Television is a unique medium that presents unique challenges to an automated lighting programmer. It is often very difficult for a programmer who works primarily with live events to switch over to television programming. Training yourself to focus your attention on the monitor and not the stage can be difficult. Just remember that the most important view is that of the camera.

MUSIC FESTIVALS AND ON-OFFS

So you have been hired to program for a 3-day music festival. What do you do? If it is like most festivals, you will be given a plot and very little other information (Figure 7.4).

Figure 7.4   Music Festivals and On-Offs Often Present Unique Situations

The first thing to do is to gather as much information as you can. Oftentimes this might mean going to the website for the event to see what acts will be on your stage. Now try to listen to some music from each of the bands to get a good understanding of what you are up against. I have seen some shows that will go from a DJ, to rap, to rock, to top-40, and then to hip-hop. You need to be prepared for anything.

Organize Your Data

Most festivals are so big that many of the details we are looking for to do our job are just not available. So you might be given a plot (you might even be designing the rig), but usually there is very little organization. The first concern you should have is your programming time. Consider yourself lucky if you get more than one night to preprogram for all 22 acts! So your first priority should be to try to gain as much programming time as possible. The best way to do this is to organize your needs and see they are taken care of at load in. If you take the time before the show to build the patch and create a plot showing all the addresses, universes, placement notes, etc. then you can shave a few hours off the load in time. I will usually take the plot I am sent and add in all the information I feel will be needed and send it back to the crew chief. In addition, I will bring 6–7 copies with me and have them ready to hand out to any crew member who might need it.

Ask for FOH power as soon as possible. This way while they are building the rig, you can make yourself busy by building your new home. Set up the consoles, monitors, UPS, etc. As soon as fixtures have power and data you want to be ready to test that everything is working correctly. Try to prepare as much of your show file as you can prior to the event. I am not talking about using visualization to preprogram the entire show (unless they are paying for your preprogramming time), but patching a show and building some groups and palettes on an offline editor should only take an hour or two. If you arrive on site with this little bit of work complete, then you can start programming as soon as the rig is ready.

Programming

Even if the rig is not complete, begin programming as soon as you can on site. Make the most of this time and program with what fixtures you do have. If you wait until the rig is 100%, then you will have very little programming time. Generally you will know little to nothing about the bands and their set lists, so you need to be prepared for anything. Try to program a page or two of looks that will allow you to deal with most situations. For example, you will need a few different stage washes, color bumps, audience looks, etc. Do not spend lots of time programming very complex effects and chases. You will find that while they might look great, it is very hard to work these types of things into varied musical acts on the fly. Instead, you might want to build things you can trigger manually so that they can work with any tempo.

One Approach

Every programmer will layout their console differently, but here is a general idea of how I do it for these situations. I will have about 8 bump buttons of color bumps, usually different colors for each fixture type stored in one button. Next I will have shutter controls where I can blackout fixtures by type. Then some ballyhoos and flyouts by type, and strobe chases by fixture type. Another 8 to 10 playbacks will be devoted to what I call "rock looks." These are big stage looks using all fixtures. When a song begins, I can play a rock look while blacking out the hard edge fixtures. Then for the chorus I can switch to blacking out the wash fixtures and see only the hard edge. On a downbeat I can switch back to the wash lights, with a different color while flying out to the audience, then restore to the hard edge in yet another color. This entire time I am playing from the one "rock look" but modifying it live and to the beat via my bump buttons. This simple approach allows me to keep the show fresh and vibrant throughout the different acts.

My approach does not allow me much time to rest during the show. I have seen operators who like to press one or two buttons during a song and not make many changes on stage. Touring productions can take the time to program a show so that a single GO button can be pressed at key moments, but with a festival gig this is usually not possible. Some slower songs might allow me a moment or two to have a drink, but generally my fingers are flying as long as the band is playing. The reasoning for my method is because with no rehearsals, there is no way to synchronize the lights to the beat, unless you play along live. In addition, this provides the best light show as it continually works with the music on stage.

Visiting LDs

Sometimes a band will arrive with their own LD, which can lead to three different scenarios. In some cases the LD will arrive the day before and ask to spend a few hours after the gates close to program his specific cues (he will probably use your positions and groups). Other LDs will get on the headset to call followspots and call cues to you, with you using whatever you have in the desk. This is where you will need common washes, colors, strobes, etc. In the final scenario, the LD will simply walk up to your desk and run it using whatever you make available. Then you can just sit back and watch the magic of someone else running your cues.

Fun for All

Festival gigs can be tremendous fun and lots of work. They give you a chance to work with many acts and varied musical types in a short amount of time. These productions can be a great place for creative experimentation and programming experience. Remember to keep it simple and have fun and you will get through all the acts with no problem.

ARCHITECTURAL INSTALLATIONS

Automated lighting is often not only used on stages and in studios, but also for permanent architectural installations. Exteriors of buildings, bridges, monuments, retail store interiors, movie theatre lobbies, and even private homes are often enhanced through the use of automated lighting. Most lighting manufacturers have answered this demand by creating fixtures and consoles specifically for this market. Just as many of the fixtures are unique, the programming of an architectural installation requires special techniques and procedures not commonly used in other programming applications (Figure 7.5).

Where Is FOH?

The placement of the lighting console for programming purposes is an extremely important decision. You will need a vantage point where you can see the majority of your lighting surface. In fact, you might require

Figure 7.5 Architectural Installations Can Run for Many Years

multiple programming positions. For example, if you are lighting a building on all four sides, you might need four programming positions. Each of these positions will need a specific setback distance that allows a wide view of the building. Power and data will need to be accessed at each of these locations, as well as a form of communication with your technical crew. Programming a large surface may require that your FOH position is hundreds or thousands of feet away. Modern lighting consoles can use fiber-optic or wireless communications to allow control from virtually anywhere.

Look at the Time

The majority of permanent architectural lighting installations run in a stand-alone mode. The console is usually programmed so the fixtures turn on and off at a preset time. In addition, cues may need to be triggered at specific times and/or dates. All this programming will usually fall to the automated lighting programmer. Most consoles have a clock allowing for cue triggers at specific times of day or days of week. Some desks also include an astronomical clock function. When you input the location of the installation via latitude and longitude, the console will calculate individual sunrise and sunset times for every single day. These calculations are very useful as they can be used with or without an offset to trigger lighting events.

In addition to programming the lighting cues, you might need to enter additional data to turn the fixtures on or off. Most fixtures have a control channel that allows for shutdown and startup of the fixture. If you build a cue to shutdown the fixtures at 5 A.M. and another cue to start them up at 6 P.M., then you can use clock triggers to automate the fixture usage. Sometimes the lighting installer will simply use a timer to enable or disable power to the lighting fixtures at a specific time. You will need to be aware of this as it might affect your programming period. There is nothing worse that programming all night long only to have power disabled to the fixtures at 4 A.M. (just when you are nearly finished).

User Interactions

Many architectural installations will simply run as programmed and require no interaction from the users. This is a good thing as there is usually not a lighting professional on staff at the location. Many times the automated lighting is looked at by the staff no differently than the parking lot or interior lights. However, even if no user interaction is expected, you should plan accordingly. First (if you are able to), lock the console functions with a password. Make backups of the show file and store them on the controller's hard drive, or at some location near the controller. This way if something goes wrong, you can point someone to a backup copy of the show file(s). In addition, you might create manually triggered functions to override the normal operation of the lighting show. For example, there might be a need to turn fixtures on or off other than during the scheduled hours. Additionally, the staff might want to override lighting looks on specific holidays (for example, red for Valentine's Day). If you have the time, it does not hurt to add these additional cue options into the programming.

More complex installations may interact with additional show control computers. These systems will trigger the lighting console (via MIDI or SMPTE, etc.) as needed. You will need to coordinate with the show control specialist to determine what type of interaction is needed.

Maintenance

As stated earlier, most architectural lighting installations generally do not have specialized lighting personnel on staff. This can be very frustrating when you return to the installation at a later date to find fixtures with burned out lamps or broken electronics. While there is little you can do to resolve hardware problems, you should try to minimize problems due to programming. For instance, if you created cues to strike and shutdown the lamps of the fixtures, you should confirm they are working correctly. No one might notice if the fixtures are burning their lamps all day, but this will reduce the lamp life of the fixtures and possibly cause overheating problems. Before completing your lighting programming, you should verify that your cueing is working as expected. In addition you might put in a secondary shutdown or startup command (10 minutes after the first), just in case something goes wrong.

Because these installations are usually not supervised by lighting professionals in the same manner as a normal production, you should program in additional safeguards. For example, you could find a moment halfway through the evening to send a reset command to the fixtures. This can help to ensure all fixtures are properly calibrated and working correctly. Instead of resetting them all at the same time, you might do it in three groups of fixtures to minimize the distraction. Small details such as this can greatly improve the overall life span of an architectural installation.

Permanent Joys

Sometimes architectural installations can be frustrating to program due to harsh conditions (programming lighting for a bridge spanning icy waters during the winter), or strange hours (entering a shopping mall as everyone else is leaving). However, these installations offer a huge reward that is often not available with other types of productions: longevity. An installation will often remain active for many years and be seen by millions of people. It is very satisfying to return after five years to an installation and see your programming still in action.

8

Troubleshooting

As the programmer of the show, you are generally not responsible for the working order of the fixtures. However, there are many times when it is necessary for you to troubleshoot the problem to help the technicians determine the exact nature of the problem. In addition, since you are the one "driving the car," all data-related problems always point back to you and the console. For example, if a light is acting sporadically and randomly blacking out, this could be related to data lines, the console, the fixture itself, or even the programming. What follows are some common problems and troubleshooting procedures that you will be faced with as a programmer.

COMMON PROBLEMS

The first step in solving problems is recognizing that you have a problem. Problems can be obvious, such as the lights do not respond to the desk at all, or subtle, such as the fixtures cannot accurately hit the same spot twice. Sometimes a fixture might flicker or shake as if it has a nervous twitch. Other times the lights seem to be running cues from a different show. Whatever the problem, you need to find the cause and repair it quickly so programming time is not lost.

DATA PROBLEMS

A good way to think of your data and data lines is as water in water pipes. If your pipes have leaks or clogs, then the water will not get through to the faucet. Generally speaking it is always a good idea to have a terminator on your data lines. A terminator is usually a resistor on pins 2 and 3 built into a male XLR connector (check your fixture's manual for exact specifications). Lack of termination can cause all kinds of wacky problems. Using the water pipe analogy, termination is like putting a plug at the end of a water line to maintain good water pressure. If the plug is not in the line, all the water spews out the end of the pipe and reduces water pressure. Lack of DMX termination can cause fixtures anywhere in the data line to act erratically. For instance, fixtures might flash on and off or oscillate their color wheel, or even not respond at all. Sometimes it might be just one fixture, sometimes more. If you have multiple data lines from your console or from a data splitter, be sure to terminate each DMX line.

The DMX-512 specifications indicate the data line run should be no more than 2500 feet. If you have extremely long cable runs, you might see problems similar to lack of termination. In addition, fixtures beyond a certain point in the data line may not respond to the DMX. The simple way to solve this problem is to put a DMX splitter in the line, as most DMX splitters also amplify the signal.

Care should be given to the DMX data cables. If the cables have a break or cut in them, some fixtures may not work. I have actually seen a data cable that had a break in pin 1. The hard edge fixtures in the rig operated correctly, yet the wash lights would not even respond. It turned out that the hard edge fixtures could operate without this part of the signal, while the wash lights could not. A faulty data cable usually causes fixtures beyond that cable not to work and is pretty easy to find. If there is a short in a data cable, this can be more difficult to find. It is always a good idea to carry a DMX tester of some type with you. There are very simple testers built into XLR connectors and very complex testers made to work with personal digital assistants (PDAs). As long as we are talking cables, with DMX it is a bad idea to make a Y cable to turn one run into two. Twofers are commonplace with electricity, but should never be used with data. DMX splitters are commonly available and should always be used to split data runs.

CONSOLE PROBLEMS

If the data lines check out okay, then you could have a problem with your console. Console troubles might be due to problems in the patch of your fixtures, so first verify that you have the correct settings in the patch and at the fixtures. In addition, you might need to use your DMX tester to analyze the output from the console. Most fixtures prefer a DMX refresh rate of around 30 MHz. If your console is refreshing at a slower rate, the lights might not behave correctly. Many consoles have fuses on the data lines to protect the console from power coming down the data lines. If one of these fuses is blown, you will not get any DMX output. Also, check with your console manufacturer to make sure the version of software you are using does not contain bugs that could affect the processing of DMX. New consoles are appearing on the market every day, and any of them could have many different types of bugs causing unexpected behavior from your console. If you suspect the console is causing the error, try sending DMX to the fixture(s) from a DMX tester or another desk and see if the problem continues.

FIXTURE PROBLEMS

If you are sure that the console is operating correctly and the data lines are good, then the problem could be with the fixture itself. The first step to test for a bad fixture would be to address another fixture of the same type to the same address as the fixture with the problem. If the problem now occurs on both fixtures, then you know the difficulty is not fixture specific. If one fixture behaves correctly and the other still responds poorly, then you need to determine what is wrong with the fixture. Notify the lighting technicians that the fixture needs to be repaired and let them know what type of problems you are seeing. If you are both the programmer and the lighting tech, then you will have to stop programming and go fix it yourself.

OPERATOR ERROR

As much as we hate to admit it, sometimes we might be the cause of the problem. If a fixture is not responding at all, maybe it has been parked from the console or sent a shutdown command. It could be as simple as not paying attention to what is currently selected on your desk. For example, if you select the "CS truss" group and find the center fixture is not responding, the problem could be because you forgot to put this fixture in that group. If a fixture appears to be randomly blacking out, maybe the console is telling it to black out and you do not realize it. I remember one show where I had a fixture that would fade to black every minute or so and I could not determine the cause. It turns out that a cuelist I built two days before to control the fogger accidentally had a value of zero on one cue for this particular fixture. Because the fogger cuelist was "running in the background" I did not immediately think to check it as the cause of the problem. The simple fix was to remove the errant value from the fogger cuelist.

Getting Help

Problems most certainly will occur and the sooner they can be resolved, the sooner you can get back to work. If you are aware of the common problems and solutions, you can help determine and solve most situations. When you are stumped and are at the end of your resources, there are usually people you can call. Our industry is very good about providing technical support. Not only do most fixture manufacturers offer 24/7 support, but also many of the lighting suppliers and production companies do as well. Before you encounter any problems, note the phone numbers you might need and carry these with you.

EMERGENCY PREPAREDNESS

Imagine this: You are standing at FOH with total control of all lighting in a venue filled with a large crowd. You are suddenly told there is a major storm outside and a tornado is rapidly approaching. What do you do next? Are you prepared for the unknown? Disasters can occur at any time without warning and as professional lighting programmers and operators, we must be prepared.

There have been many major nightclub and other production-related tragedies throughout history. Part of the problem in these situations resulted from entertainment professionals not being prepared for the unexpected. If everyone involved in a production were to maintain a high level of safety standards, then fewer accidents would occur. I believe there are procedures and plans that lighting programmers should consider as professionals to assist in these situations. Since I have been involved with this industry for more than 15 years, I have had some experiences that have taught me valuable lessons. However, I still try to prepare for the unknown and be ready to handle any situation.

Be Prepared

Early in my career, I was running followspot for a country act at an outdoor amphitheater when we were told by the LD to lock down our spots and get down off the roof ASAP. We then noticed a huge wall cloud approaching and heard tornado sirens. Once we got down on stage, we discovered the power to the venue had been cut off. The two wimpy emergency lights on stage worked only for about 10 minutes. I was shocked to find I was one of the few stagehands on the call with a flashlight (two actually) in my bag. Not only did we have to begin load-out in the dark, we also had to deal with a hostile crowd that could not leave the venue (the parking lots were flooded with four feet of water). Since that event, I have always made it a point to have a flashlight in my pocket for *every* show I am working. In addition, I check the batteries periodically and carry a spare flashlight in my bag. You never know when something will go wrong, and if anyone should have a flashlight at the ready, it is the lighting guy.

Safety of Others

As the lighting operator, you are responsible for the lighting inside the venue. If there is a major incident in the crowd, you might have to bring up audience lights to help emergency personnel. I saw footage of a festival where several audience members were crushed by the swelling crowd. In the news footage, I could see all the stage lights in open white pointing into the crowd. The lighting operator was extremely helpful to the medical and security personnel. To prepare for these types of situations, you should have a "work light" cue ready to bring up at any time (during rehearsals and performances). If you are in the middle of programming and you hear a loud crash and yell, you should be able to instantly access this cue to help ascertain what just happened. In the same manner, you need to be sensitive to others who might be working while you are programming. If there are technicians on stage and in the rig, you might not want to trigger your strobe lights. I am usually very aware of other people when working with a large number of strobe lights. I often call out "Watch your eyes, the strobes are about to fire" just before I test a strobe cue. This way if a technician is staring right at the center of a strobe, he will not be blinded (or at least he was warned!).

Personal Safety

I make it a point to ask for security barricades and personnel for my FOH position. You never know who may try to get up to your position. Not only will they distract you from your work, but they could also cause problems. Even if you are working in a theatre, you will want to ensure there is restricted access to the lighting booth. If your console is set up on a riser or road cases, you will want to double-check that everything is locked down. Imagine what could happen if the entire FOH was to collapse without notice. You should always take the time to confirm you have a safe working environment.

Even before the terrible events of September 11, we had to deal with security checks and bomb searches. Now the threats are much more credible and convincing. If you feel a particular event is not secure enough, then you should say something or not do the gig. I know of several programmers who turned down jobs on New Year's Eve 2000 simply because they felt the personal security risk was too great. In addition, if you notice some other hazard (poor rigging, unsafe pyrotechnics, etc.) you need to consider your options. If you accept the danger, you could put yourself and others at risk. You should also think about the possibility that you could be held responsible in a court of law if you are part of a production involving a major accident.

The Actor's Point of View

Many years ago when I was running the lighting for a production of *Annie*, I made a big mistake. During a performance, I jumped the gun and took a blackout early. This resulted in a child actor falling off a riser on the set and twisting her ankle. I felt terrible, as I knew that I had directly caused her injury. When programming and operating the lighting in a venue, you must consider the performers on stage. Walk up on the stage and see how blinding the cues you just built are from center stage. You might find that the angles of the floor fixtures do not allow the performers to see the front edge of the stage. This could lead you to update your positioning to a better angle. In addition, consider what the actors are doing. For example, when programming lighting for ice skating events, it is common practice to light the ice bright with no cues or changes when you expect the skaters to perform jumps. If you were to take a cue at the same instant a jump is to occur, it could be disastrous for the skater. In the same manner you should consider the audience's point of view as well. When projecting textures on the walls of a venue you should check to see that patrons are not blinded going up and down steps or in and out of doorways.

Safety First

As professionals in the entertainment industry, we must take responsibility for our area of specialization. We should do everything we can to ensure that all elements relating to the lighting are the safest they can be, and that we have prepared for every possible contingency. By imagining the worst, we only help to make the show the best it can be. Think of any production related tragedy in history and imagine you were there. If you were standing at FOH behind the lighting console at the moment of the disaster, how would you have reacted?

9

Programmer and Designer Relationships

Working as a professional Lighting Programmer requires many skills beyond programming of lights. The relationship between a programmer and an LD is oftentimes more important than how well either one can handle his individual job. One of the most amazing things in our profession is how a group of people who have never met before can come together and make a show a success in a short amount of time. The working relationships become just as important as the knowledge and skill of those involved. The first time we work with a designer, we must quickly determine how he or she works, their personality, their quirks, etc. Oftentimes there is very little time to "get to know" the people you are working with, as production schedules are too tight.

PEOPLE ARE PEOPLE

When arriving at a gig or meeting an LD for the first time, you must remember that everyone is there for the same goal: To make the show a success. You might make a new best friend with the LD and have a great career programming all his or her shows. However, you might also find that the LD has annoying habits that drive you so crazy that you just want to leave the gig. Of course, you do not leave the gig, but you find that the LD might be difficult to work with. This is where your relationship skills will be put to the test. If you can learn to recognize the different types of LDs and quickly adapt to their lighting style and personality, then you will be successful in most situations. Even if you cannot stand the person you are working with, you must endure and make the show a success. Then you can go home and never work with that LD again.

TYPES OF LDS

I have found that there are four basic relationships between an LD and a programmer. If you can learn to work with each type, then you can handle most any situation. Learning to read LDs to determine how they work can be difficult if you have never worked with them before. Of course, all these relationships assume that you know your console and your fixtures extremely well and are talented with your craft.

1. **A perfect collaboration**—The LD and the programmer work together bouncing ideas off each other to create the end product. The ideas for looks come from both, while the programmer will carry out the actual execution; both will take part in the creative process before, during, and after the initial programming. The LD usually draws the plot but looks to the programmer for suggestions or changes. During preproduction both the LD and the programmer have equal input into the creative process of the show. This is the most common situation, as it results in the best final product for the production.

2. **The LD rules**—The LD knows what he or she wants and simply tells the programmer what to build. The programmer is just an extension of the LD executing the commands that the LD does not have the time or knowledge to do. The programmer does not provide much creative input and is purely there for data entry. During preproduction the LD will call out the looks and the programmer will simply input the data into the desk. The programmer might offer some suggestions, but the LD decides the overall looks. In this scenario, the programmer oftentimes has to refrain from comment and just build the cues the way the LD suggests, even if the programmer has other ideas.

3. **The LD rests**—The LD hands over most creative aspects to the programmer. The programmer will come up with and build the looks. The LD may suggest a few changes when looking at the finished

product, but trusts whatever the programmer wants to create. During preproduction, the LD might offer a suggestion or direction for a song or scene, but leaves the cue creation process to the programmer.

4. **The LD and the co-LD**—The programmer is actually working in conjunction with the LD to design the show. Usually only the programmer will input the data to the desk, but both the LD and the co-LD consult with each other on every lighting decision made. Both have equal decision-making responsibilities and both must interact directly with the artist/client to ensure the overall vision of the show. This is very similar to number one, yet a little different, as both are working as LDs.

TROUBLED WATERS

Some LDs might have trouble focusing on the task at hand and may be very busy working on other shows, conducting business on the cell phone, or meeting with the artist or client. Others will let their creative juices flow and sit with you for hours painting with light, putting off everything else during the programming session. You must learn to cope with all different situations and adapt instantly. If the LD has to step away to make a phone call, you have a choice to make. You can sit back and wait for him to return, you can press on building looks, or you can do "desk cleanup" (labeling, organizing, etc. within the console). Some LDs will want to be involved with the look-making process (after all they are the LDs), others would rather have you wait, while some will appreciate your pressing on or cleaning up the console.

CHANGING TIDES

Of course, any given LD will behave differently with different shows. As each show has its own sets of constraints and the stress level changes, so will yours and the LD's personalities. For example, I have worked with an LD on a concert tour where we had 2 weeks of preproduction. The LD had lots of time to spend with me at the desk building looks. I built very few cues without him next to me providing input. Then I worked with the same LD on a live TV shoot with only 18 hours from load-in to on-air. He was so busy running around focusing conventionals, talking with directors and choreographers, etc. that he had very little time to make any lighting look decisions. I had to quickly take charge and build the show myself. Then during a very stressed rehearsal he would give me notes over the headsets to finesse the cues he felt needed adjusting. I had to quickly realize the difference between the two shows and understand how our working relationship would change. Had I just sat and waited during the TV shoot, then there would have been no lighting for the rehearsal.

LIFE IS LIKE A BOX OF CHOCOLATES

Life requires a certain amount of psychology, and lighting programming is no exception. Working many hours with no sleep, staring at a stage with lights flashing in your eyes can create all kinds of stress and test even the best of friends. There are many different circumstances and personalities in our industry and I have tried to focus on the most common. We must learn to evaluate each situation and respond in a professional manner and remember the success of the show is the most important factor.

10

Digital Lighting, the Future Is Here

Ten years ago while attending a lighting convention, I sat in on a discussion of the newest innovations in automated lighting technology. At the end of the seminar I remember a well-respected LD was asked what he thought the Holy Grail of automated lighting was. He said that in the next ten to fifteen years all lights will be digital. He described a system where instead of using mechanical functions and glass to change the output of a fixture, everything will be generated in a video-like format. These digital lighting fixtures would be more than just a video projector on a yoke, as they would contain specific software to enable them to behave as lighting fixtures. Any image, any texture, any color could be projected with no limits. I was thrilled by this vision and hoped it would come true sooner than later.

Here we are ten years later and this technology is finally emerging within our industry. Sure, many have tried in the past, but there have been various problems. The first problem is brightness. Video projections are currently created using one of two methods. The first uses a liquid crystal display (LCD) screen, which light is shined through to cast an image on a surface. The other method is called Digital Light Processing (DLP). Texas Instruments created DLP by using a microchip built with hundreds of tiny mirrors. When a light is focused on this surface and the mirrors are turned on and off, they project the pixels of a video image. Video projector manufacturers must work with these methods to optimize the output from a lamp without burning up their technology. Currently the brightest (and largest) video projectors output around 20,000 lumens, while midsized projectors are about 5000 lumens. Compare this with approximately 9000 lumens of a standard 575 watt moving light and you will see the complications.

The other hurdle automated lighting manufacturers have had to overcome is the programming interface for digital lighting fixtures. In the last few years we have seen several products come to market that allow for direct DMX control and manipulation of video sources, images, and various content formats. Automated lighting programmers need to be aware of this new frontier and begin to learn more about file formats, content creation, and other digital products.

CONTENT

It is important to remember that although we are talking about video technology, the use is very different. Much of the terminology and concepts, however, are new to the lighting industry. First there is content. Instead of gobos, prisms, and other effects, digital lights make use of various computer files to playback their imagery. These movies, photographs, animations, etc. are referred to as content or media, and content is one of the most important elements of a digital light. As important as good gobos are for standard lighting fixtures, the same is true for content. Think about being able to project anything you desire onto your stage. Great, now where will you get that content? You will either need to create it, have it made, or purchase it. Luckily the video industry has demanded content for years, so there is a lot of it available for purchase.

Digital lighting programmers may find it important to be skilled in content creation and editing. I know of many programmers who are beginning to take classes in computer-based video editing and animation creation. Currently, if a programmer is able to create and modify content while also programming the show, then the programmer is that much more desirable. However, there comes a point when a lighting programmer must focus on programming and not content creation and editing. As we head into this new frontier it will be interesting to see who is required to provide and edit the content. Will the rental companies need to have a stock of computer files they can load into the digital lights they rent? Will lighting designers or even lighting programmers need to supply the content? Maybe an entire new profession will be created with production staff allocated to content design and creation. It is an exciting time in our industry, as the next few years will shape the standards and methods for the future.

NEW JOBS

Wait! Did I say automated lighting programmers will be better off if they know how to create and modify content? Presently the lighting programmer does not have to know how to create or install gobos on moving lights, so why does he or she need to know content creation? Right now you will find that most shows using digital lighting will have the lighting programmer look after the computers, software, and media of the digital lights. This is because the fixture technicians are not familiar with the technology and the lighting programmer is also usually a computer guru. Furthermore, the lighting programmer interacts directly with the content via DMX, so it's only natural that he or she is familiar with the digital lighting software and content creation. So right now, at this moment in this technology's history, it is important for a digital lighting programmer to be familiar with the product's software as well as content creation. Someone else on the production staff **should** provide and edit the content prior to its manipulation via DMX, but this is not always the case. I always remind people that I am a lighting programmer and not a content creator/editor. If I have to stop programming the lighting to rerender a movie file, then I am losing time behind the console.

Over the next five years I think we will see several new production positions created. First there will be digital content specialists. These people will create and modify content specific to a production's needs. They may simply be custom content providers or they may be media designers working directly with the lighting and production designers. In addition, there will initially be a need for specialized digital lighting technicians. Besides maintaining the actual fixtures (changing lamps, adjusting DLP or LCD components, etc.) they will also be responsible for loading content into the fixtures' computers or servers. Over time I predict all lighting technicians will gain the knowledge and experience, thus negating the specialist title. Both of the above positions will enable the lighting programmer to concentrate on simply programming the lights, digital or otherwise. Ultimately there will be conventionals, automated lights, and digital lights, and a good lighting programmer will be able to program any of them interchangeably. However, right now if lighting programmers want to become involved in this exciting new technology, they will have to be prepared to fill the shoes of all the positions I have listed previously.

POINT OF VIEW

We now have three distinct types of lighting equipment: conventional, automated, and digital. Many uninformed individuals look at the new digital projection technology as a simple marriage of lighting and video. They are quick to dismiss the technology as straightforward video editing that can be accomplished with common video production tools. On the other hand, many visionaries perceive the technologies as another new lighting tool. In fact, it has the potential of being the ultimate lighting tool. When approached as a lighting fixture, the possibilities are endless. For example, we now have digital lights, digital gobos, digital backdrops, digital beamage, and countless other effects. No longer are we limited by mechanical functions such as gears, dichroics, motors, and belts. Every element projected out of a fixture is created digitally via a computer. When you can look beyond basic video functionality and into the creative digital world, then you are ready to begin exploring digital lighting.

SERVERS AND DISPLAY DEVICES

Currently modern digital lighting technology consists of two main elements. The first is a media server. This computer houses all the content and generates all the manipulations as directed by DMX input. The second essential component is the display device. Video projectors, plasma screens, LED video walls, computer monitors, and other similar devices make up this category. In the future we will see complete digital lighting fixtures that house both a server and projector in one simple unit. Until then we must continue to have both elements in separate locations. If you are using a large number of media servers, you might find it best to locate these backstage and run video cables to the output devices. Now you will have created a "Digital Beach" right alongside of "Dimmer Beach."

NEW FUNCTIONALITY AND TERMINOLOGY

Currently there are only a few digital lighting products on the market. Each has its own approach to content manipulation; however, they all share some common parameters. First is content selection. A digital lighting product must allow the programmer to select items for playback. With standard automated lights, there are gobo wheels which usually contain 6–8 gobos. Choosing gobos is a simple process of selecting a gobo wheel and a gobo. A very similar process is used for choosing content with digital lighting. Instead of wheels, content is stored in *folders*, *banks*, and *libraries*. Then within each a *file*, *image*, or *source* can be chosen. Once a file is selected for playback, the *play mode* or *playback* parameter can be altered to define the order in which content portions (or frames) are viewed. Some options include loop forward, loop reverse, random play, play once forward, pause, and stop.

A good digital lighting product will first set out to duplicate the functionality of an automated lighting fixture. It should have functions we are all familiar with, such as intensity, color mixing, iris, framing shutters, strobe, image rotation, frost, and zoom to name a few. There are, of course, many other parameters that are unique to digital lighting. It is imperative that automated lighting programmers learn this new vocabulary and become familiar with its uses within digital lighting. Some of the terminology as used by today's various products are defined next.

Aspect: A parameter that allows modifying the geometry of an image to change its relationship between height and width of the content and manipulations.

Frame Rate: The speed at which content is played back. Usually displayed in frames per second (fps).

Keystone: A function that allows altering the geometry of an image to alter its shape. Very useful for correcting images projected at extreme angles. This functionality usually consists of 4 to 6 parameters for total geometry correction.

Layer: A different series of effects and/or content that can be overlaid with other content to create a single output. Each layer generally has its own set of controls that alter only that layer. Similar to multiple gobo wheels within an automated lighting fixture.

Mask: Content that is used to block visibility of another layer. The mask is usually on a separate layer from the main content. Often used to create output similar to a gobo or iris of an automated lighting fixture.

Position: The location of content and manipulations within the raster can be altered on both horizontal (X) and vertical (Y) axes.

Raster: The area of active video as output from the media server. This boundary is defined by the resolution of the media server's computer.

Scale: Similar to a zoom function of an automated lighting fixture, this parameter will change the size of the output within the raster.

Shape: Allows for applying or wrapping content and manipulations around a 3D object or 2D shape.

Trails: An effect that adds slowly fading out "ghosting" of images. Especially noticeable when rotating images or moving them within the raster.

X rotation: Allows for indexing and rotation of content and manipulations around a horizontal axis in 3D space.

Y rotation: Allows for indexing and rotation of content and manipulations around a vertical axis in 3D space.

Z rotation: Allows for indexing and rotation of content and manipulations on a flat plane in 2D space. Very similar to standard gobo rotations of an automated lighting fixture.

PROGRAMMING DIGITAL LIGHTING

Now is an exhilarating period in lighting history, as this technology is in its infancy. However, this can also be frustrating, as there are no standards, common methods, or similar terminology between products. Luckily the one common element with these fixtures is DMX control. All the programming is the same as any standard automated light, using the console of your choice. I suggest you think of these products as you would any other new fixture and first study the DMX protocol. Once you learn how the "aspect" parameter alters the content output from the fixture, then you can relate all your normal programming knowledge to this new parameter type. If you begin to get lost in the new terminology and are worried that you do not understand the manipulations, step back and remember it is just a digital moving light controlled by DMX. These products are very simple from a lighting programmer's point of view, as they do not require any special programming talents.

It is thrilling to apply lighting techniques to a new medium. For example, think of using a digital lighting server to control the imagery on an upstage wall. You have now created a "digital backdrop" or "digital cyc." This technology allows you to have any image you desire and manipulate it from your lighting desk. So instead of simply fading out the backdrop, you can program the imagery to fade to blue while scaling (zooming) and dimming out. The combined "lighting programming" will be viewed as new "animation" on the backdrop. The difference is that this magic was created with the same keystrokes and skills you have used on every show.

ENOUGH IS ENOUGH

With standard automated lights, there are X number of gobos and X number of effects. By combining the various parameters, you can create a certain number of looks. However, because the possibilities with digital lighting are endless you must first decide what content is best for your needs. Then you must decide when your manipulation of the content is enough. With digital lighting, you have the ability to control such a multitude of parameters that it can become difficult to determine which is best. Remember, there are few mechanical limits to hold back your creativity, which can be both a hindrance and a blessing.

THE FUTURE IS NOW

We have come a long way from a simple ellipsoidal with one gobo and one color to the cutting edge of digital lighting where we can project and manipulate anything we desire. In addition to controlling the output from projectors, we are now able to directly control the content on video walls, plasma screens, etc. I look forward to the exciting lighting revolution that is only just beginning!

11

Words of Wisdom from Industry Professionals

In the business of automated lighting programming, experience can make or break a good programmer. Throughout my years of programming I have learned from every designer and programmer I work with. I continue to learn with each new production. I asked many of my colleagues to share any advice they would like to pass on to others regarding programming of automated lighting.

ADRIAN NGIENG, PROGRAMMER

Be humble. Learning from the great ones in your life will not stop. Learn new things. Automated lighting is not just swinging the lights but being creative and making full usage of the functions and creating the most beautiful scene you can imagine. As for a programmer, the most important things that you have to know are that your console is 100% operational and the functions of the fixtures that you are programming. With those skills nothing will stop you from creating scenes that you can imagine. Last, but not least, PRACTICE MAKES PERFECT!

ARNOLD SERAME, DESIGNER AND PROGRAMMER

If you don't like being away from home and working long evening hours under adverse conditions and sometimes intense pressure, then GET OUT NOW! And don't listen to negative people. Just because you can do it all doesn't mean you can. Listen to what the material is telling you to do. Don't create lightshows. Create lighting for the show. Keystrokes are only the beginning and the least important part of what you have to learn. Study music to learn structure and how to anticipate what a musician will do onstage. Study writing for structure, and storytelling. Study architecture for shape, space, and form. Study painting for color, light, and shadow. Study the kinds of things the people you want to work with study so that you can talk to them as an equal. Study what you're passionate about and make it a part of what you create. Remember joy. People like working with people who really enjoy what they do. Make it easy for people to work with you. Make it easy for people to call you for that next job. Concentrate on the gig you're on. Throughout your career, have faith in the following maxim: There aren't enough good people to do what needs to be done. Somewhere out there, some artist, director, manager, lighting company, and/or production manager, is looking for the next hot lighting person, which naturally leads to the next directive: Make it easy for people to find you. And this above all: Throughout your career, keep on refinding that sense of magic and wonder that brought you to lighting in the first place.

BENOIT RICHARDS, DESIGNER AND PROGRAMMER

The key to a successful production is simple: You have to know and understand the main subject of what you are going to light; especially for the concert industry, where you should listen to the songs over and over, before you can even start to program the cues. Months before I program a tour, I listen to the songs in my car so many times that all the intros, accents, and endings are subconsciously printed in my mind. Once I know what's going on in each song, I'll sit down and "chart" each moment (cue) and basically create the first draft of my show cuelist. With an offline editor, I immediately enter those blank cues in the main list. Then, when I arrive at production rehearsals, my extensive knowledge of the material will flow naturally from my thoughts, through the console, and make sense of each part of the song I am trying to light.

BRYAN HARTLEY, DESIGNER AND PROGRAMMER

Things are totally different than they were when I started, yet they are the same. Find a young band or start with a lighting company. These days everyone has moving lights so your imagination is your best tool. Also, video is a great tool, especially when the lighting designer has control and can use it as a light as well as imaging.

BUD HOROWITZ, DESIGNER AND PROGRAMMER

Very often my programming time is extremely limited, hours instead of days. I frequently do not know enough about the content of the event or the music of the entertainer(s) performing. The first thing that I do is to spend a significant amount of available time building as diverse an amount of palettes as possible. Once the building blocks are there, creation of the "looks" is so much more simplified. Not having the luxury of time, much of the "process of discovery" must come in the building of palletized focuses.

BUTCH ALLEN, DESIGNER AND PROGRAMMER

Stay away from drugs. Drugs do not make anyone more creative and are just a waste of time, money, and brain cells. If you are going to tour, you must be willing to give up everything and live on a bus. So to prepare, you should avoid showering for a week, while wearing the same shirt and shorts. Behave as a professional as this is a business, and save your money for when your career ends.

CHRISTIAN CHOI, PROGRAMMER

The three most important things you will need to keep in mind when building the infrastructure of your show are consistency, efficiency, and organization. With time and experience you'll learn what infrastructure you really need to start a show with and you'll relax about spending too much time on building things you might find redundant later.

DALL BROWN, DESIGNER

Remember that lighting design is about art *supported by technology*. A designer has to have good artistic vision *and* well-organized technical skills. All too often in the rush of daily work we lose sight of the art and let the technology drive our decisions. Whether we are lighting an intimate scene with one candle or a multiscene show with hundreds of lights, we need to be able to keep the creative vision alive and let it guide the design process.

On the practical side, lighting design demands flexibility and a willingness to adapt. You may find yourself lighting a ballet, a museum, and a trade show booth all at the same time. Each one has a different team of collaborators with a different way of working, and all have demanding schedules. An ability to stay calm and organized under stress is essential, as is the ability to get along well with a wide variety of personality types.

DAVID CHANCE, DESIGNER

After growing up in the lighting industry, and having observed ongoing evolutions of equipment and control, I believe that the next decade will offer us a level of control and functionality not conceived by most. New technologies, not yet integrated into our industry, will finally allow for real intelligent lighting to exist.

DEMFIS FYSSICOPULOS, PROGRAMMER

Do not only learn the "hows," "whats," and "whys" of a console, but also seek a good understanding and experience of the inner working of automated fixtures. In addition, due to the fast integration of networking, visualization applications, and lighting desks, a solid foundation on computers and networking I consider a true necessity. Finally, I cannot emphasize enough the importance of education. Although this is a trade traditionally based on experience, technical education will teach you a way of thinking. Schooling time will never go underestimated in this or any profession.

ERIC KENNEDY, PROGRAMMER

Always try to strive to do well at what you do, to recognize your strengths and weaknesses, and try to always keep seeking inspiration and excellence. Always take the time to look at and analyze the light plots you work on, to look at an LD's work, and try to understand both the equipment and how he used it. Everything you see and learn will help you to form your own style, and don't be afraid to copy what you like—you certainly won't be the first and that is the first step toward finding your own voice. And just as you can learn from others, you need to look at your own work and think what could be better.

ESTEBAN LIMA, DESIGNER

Don't be afraid. The technology can be daunting, but it's really there to help you. No one is going to think ill of you if you ask for help or advice, because that's the way most of us have learned. Take the work opportunities as they come. The worst that could happen is that you'll learn something new, and if you don't get that same gig again, you'll use your new knowledge in the next one. Be nice, be very nice, this especially among your peers; remember, a lot of the work you will get will come to you through recommendations, which are based, among other things, on your reputation. Nobody wants to work with people who can't get along.

Use all the resources available to you, read the manuals, read this book and keep it close to you. Make yourself a student all the time; do research when you have free time at home. Keeping your knowledge up-to-date will give you an edge—you will be surprised at how many variables there are in our industry that affect the technology we use.

HEATH MARRINAN, DESIGNER AND PROGRAMMER

Don't fall into bad habits because of laziness. What I mean is, if you are wasting time while you're programming and you know what the solution is to make your programming more efficient, then stop and take the time to fix it. When an LD is shouting out programming instructions, it is a programmer's job to make those tasks happen in a timely manner. That is why I stress just before we set the board up before our tour or show. To make tasking faster, we can always make small changes that save huge amounts of time.

Also try and challenge yourself instead of doing things you already know how to do. You won't learn if you don't try and make your time with the console as valuable as you can. So make sure you throw some tough tasks in there so you are better rounded with the console.

HENRY M. SUME, DESIGNER AND PROGRAMMER

I am constantly surprised and fascinated by the evolving nature of being a programmer. Today's programmer is much more of an integral part of the lighting team than even just a few years ago. Where shows used to be mostly conventional with maybe a handful of automation thrown in for "flash and trash," now the opposite is true. The automated fixtures are carrying more and more of the workload of creating and sustaining the visual feel of the show.

As a programmer, you'll often find yourself acting as one big interface. It's your job to translate a designer's language into a language that the console understands. Further, you have to translate between the way the console operates and the way your specific fixtures operate. That's not to say that the role of programmer is artless. Far from it— oftentimes as a programmer you have a much more direct influence on the visual impact of the show than just about anyone else involved. That said, while you're working on a show, the greatest skill you can have is knowing when to discuss things and give your opinions and when to just shut up and punch the buttons. Whenever possible, STAY BEHIND THE CONSOLE! A programmer is no good to anybody if no one can find you when they need you.

HILLARY KNOX, PROGRAMMER

Lots of designers depend on programmers for creative input. When this is required, do something original; create something that everyone hasn't seen before. Now, this doesn't have to be a groundbreaking never-before-seen idea in lighting design, it can be a simple twist on something that you know that will work, but take every opportunity to try something new.

Time is always a factor in lighting. Ninety-seven times out of a hundred, you'll be under some sort of pressure to work quickly. Ten times out of a hundred, you'll be under intense, submarine captain torpedo-in-the-water pressure. It's one of the harshest realities that you just have to learn to deal with. If this is the kind of thing that you just can't deal with, then maybe programming (as a career) isn't going to be your thing. Not to sound discouraging, but if your job is going to make you intensely stressed-out on a regular basis, you have to ask yourself if it's *really* worth it.

Unfortunately, time management is one of those skills that can't really be taught, but fortunately, for most people it improves with experience. If you're in the heat of battle and have no time to think about anything except the mechanics of programming, I find that it's probably best to let the designer manage your time for you. At that moment, your job is to complete the current task, while the designer, who has the ultimate responsibility for the completion of the design, has to keep the big picture in mind at all times. Because the designer has this responsibility, he or she can (should) keep an eye on the clock and make presumably intelligent decisions about how much time should be spent on a particular cue before moving on to the next.

JIM LENAHAN, DESIGNER

The most important time a touring Lighting Designer will spend is in programming before the start of the tour. Ninety percent of the looks on the last show of the tour will be ones that were developed during that time. But it is also the hardest time to convince managers to pay for. The reason is simple. Money is going out for lighting equipment, crew, and stage rental and nothing is coming in. A friend of mine who is a film Director of Photography once told me something, which I think also applies to live touring. He said, "How good a show looks depends on how well it is lit. How well it is lit depends on how much time is spent on lighting and time costs money. That is why making shows look good is expensive." This certainly applies to programming and it is the hardest thing to make managers understand. But every extra programming day you can pry out of them will be worth its weight in gold.

JOHN BRODERICK, DESIGNER

Designers are interpreters, translating conceptual ideas into visual space. Knowing the language of ideas and the vocabulary of vision, just as a vocal interpreter is a fluent linguist, is a fundamental requirement for a designer and a programmer. Lights are tools. Don't let the tools govern you. Always refer back to the central concept of the project you are involved in. Study art, study music, study color theory. And not just the scientific theories; study the metaphysical and occult interpretations of vision and color. For example, why is there no equivalent of musical perfect pitch in the field of color vision? Why do two colors projected form a third color, but no two notes played together form a third note? Does the comprehension of light require a higher level of consciousness than humans have evolved to?

Only through the study of different disciplines and the ability to fluidly move through them can designers and programmers release themselves from the harness of technology and rise to the level of art.

JOHN RAYMENT, DESIGNER

What folks who watch shows remember about the lighting is the pictures we create. Not the hardware but the Light. Lighting is a *performed* design—and many designs today rather demand a computer (or two or nine) to run the "performance." Enter the Programmer: the designer's vital associate. There is an unspoken contract between the designer and the programmer(s)—we *need* each other (and the lighting design needs both of us).

What do I seek from a programmer? Above all, a genuine interest in the lighting—there is a distinct difference in working to achieve a design rather than playing with a console; and then the basic stuff like real competency in the console. It is your job to know your equipment—and the smarts to know what you don't know; and, please, the human comes before the machine. The effects generator is a tool, not a creator.

Lighting designs have personality and the rapport between designer and programmer will have a substantial bearing on the final result. If we are enjoying the mutual challenge and context of the pictures we are creating, then the chances of a happy result are greatly increased. And the final 10% is always the hardest to achieve.

LARRY "UNCLE FESTER" ROBBINS, DESIGNER AND PROGRAMMER

Anyone can learn a board, no one can teach that person how to program and be creative. Too many people think just because they learn a console, that makes them a programmer. They miss the most important aspects:

1. Knowing the lights, their functions, and how/what to light;
2. Knowing a good variety of boards and controllers; and

3. Most important being able to cope with the pressures of no time, crazy producers, clients, or lighting directors.

LAURA FRANK, PROGRAMMER

Stay humble, especially when you are getting started. The desire to exaggerate one's level of work experience to get those precious first jobs should not translate into attitude when faced with challenges on-site. After nearly ten years of programming, I have to occasionally pause and learn something new. Those are usually the days I enjoy most. Also, before you become dependent on fancy effects engines, make sure you've at least had the opportunity to write a 30-step offset ballyhoo on an Expression 2X. Understanding what the top of the line desks have evolved from is essential to being exceptional in your career.

LAWRENCE UPTON, DESIGNER

It is important to establish a relationship with your programmer and his requirements. Do as much homework as possible on your knowledge of the instruments. Above all, be patient. Work to establish your overall aims and then work from there. Understand that too much information at one time may slow the process down. The prohibitive cost of having a lighting system available to you in a facility is the most valuable time you will have. It is important to work on a time schedule that will give you enough time to cover all the elements you need to light.

MARSHA STERN, DESIGNER

The first thing I like to do when beginning a program for automated lights is to visualize the entire sequence of events. Sometimes I just close my eyes and visualize the way I want everything to look. Then I break down the look into its respective segments, the building blocks so to speak. I like to think of the lighting cues as bits of animation. It may take many cues to create the overall look or desired effect just as it takes many drawings to create movement from the animated character.

It is not always necessary to move/flash the lights to create an exciting visual effect. The "less is more" policy is one that I subscribe to. Truly we can best notice the movement when it is next to stillness just as we take notice of the color and light more when it is next to darkness. I think that contrast is an important concept in dynamic programming.

MATS KARLSON, PROGRAMMER

Before programming anything, make sure you know your fixtures. Understand what they can and cannot do. Every fixture has its strengths and shortcomings, and much valuable time can be wasted trying to program something that the fixture can't perform. Reading the fixture manual and spec sheet helps, but spending a little playing around with the fixtures is even better.

MICHAEL NEVITT, PROGRAMMER

LDs request the same programmers over and over. Mainly because of three factors: personality, speed, and creativity. It is hard to teach how to be personable, low stress, etc., you have it or not. Programming speed can be learned if you have the ability. Creativity is a natural part of some. If you have the ability, it can be refined. Learn the art of lighting first. Build a strong background in art, architecture, music, theatre, dance, photography, etc. A great programmer has the not-so-common ability to balance between the artistic and technical. Maintain that balance.

MIKE FALCONER, PROGRAMMER

Save, save, and save again. Never save over your backups and always have way more backups than you could ever need. Always be paranoid about your show data.

Do your homework. Know what lights you are using, how they work and how (and if) your console can handle them. A little homework goes a long way.

Get proper training on your console of choice. Talk to the manufacturer or distributor and take the time to learn the console well. No matter how good the manual is, nothing beats sitting down with someone who knows the console well and can answer your questions *and* make suggestions about what might work better.

As a rule, the lighting is there to enhance what's going on onstage. You should always have the best interests of the show at heart and the person who has employed you—light the money!

MITCH PEEBLES, PROGRAMMER

I like to hold back on effects like strobing and even movement. Just because a fixture has pan and tilt capabilities doesn't mean the fixtures need to be moving all the time. Sometimes the best lighting is lighting you don't notice.

PATRICK DIERSON, DESIGNER AND PROGRAMMER

About a month before I officially went freelance, I had a conversation with one of the most respected lighting programmers in the industry. He bestowed upon me some of the best advice that I was ever given in regards to this business. He said, "Always make sure that you've got some 'F. U. Money' so you don't have to take any small gig that you get offered just to pay your rent that month. That way when someone tries to push you into doing a really stupid gig at a stupid price because they think that they can manipulate you, simply tell them … 'F. U.' " One of my favorite quotes comes from Paul Stanley of KISS. He once said, "The only thing that having money allows you to do is not worry about money." For someone about to start out as a freelancer, I suggest that you put away enough cash to support yourself without work for approximately three months. If you play your cards right, then you should never have to invade all of those funds, but the comfort of knowing that it's there is an added bonus to an otherwise scary step in your life. It will allow you to concentrate on cultivating new business instead of selling yourself scared. Always remember that this is a business in every way. You'll need to budget your funds and time as well as market yourself as if you were a large corporation. Good luck and always remember to have fun!

PAUL PELLETIER, PROGRAMMER

The planning is very important, get all the information you can weeks before you start the actual programming: fixture type, controller type, user manual for all the equipment used. Specify in advance all the settings for the fixtures like DMX address, mode, and special fixture personality settings.

RICHARD BELLIVEAU, AUTOMATED LIGHTING INVENTOR AND VISIONARY

A few moments of darkness programmed into a show at just the right time can be more dramatic than the best lighting money can buy.

SCOTT RILEY, PROGRAMMER

When going into production, there are many things that you can have prepared as a programmer to make your sessions as time efficient as possible. Starting off with an organized approach to your palettes, groups, and even user numbers can have a substantial impact on what you are able to achieve with the limited time that is usually available to program a show. It is fairly common to keep a library of all the palettes that one creates per fixture type for the control desks regularly used. This way setup of the desk for each show can be expedited by utilizing the palettes created for previous projects. The key here is to organize them in a fashion that allows you to have all the tools available to you without taking up too much real estate. Combining like colors together into palettes for multiple types of fixtures as well as placing similar functions together such as strobing or gobo rotations can allow for more dynamic control while preserving space at the same time.

SHANNON JANUARY, DESIGNER AND PROGRAMMER

There's no such thing as an intelligent light, there's only stupid equipment and intelligent programming. Don't be afraid to do less. Just because a fixture has dozens of attributes and features doesn't mean you have to use them. Doing too much in a cue tends to diffuse the impact of a moment. On the button of a number, do all of your fixtures need to bump color and sweep to center? Will just a color bump do, or just the sweep? If the moment needs both a sweep and a bump, sweep one group or type of fixture, and color bump another.

Painting cool pictures on stage is the easy part. If you can turn the board on and grab a fixture, odds are you can create a good look. The challenge of good programming is transitioning from one great look to another and having it look good in between. Do that and you'll spend more nights in hotel beds than your own.

STEVE GARNER, PROGRAMMER

Get as much hands on experience as you can, whether it's a couple of hours at your local rental shop or a demo room or even forsaking lunch to play with lights during a load in. Also, most programmers, if they are not deep in the process (and you will know when they are), are happy to answer questions. Make yourself known as someone who is interested and more experience may follow.

STEVE IRWIN, DESIGNER AND PROGRAMMER

Programming is the technical art of converting one's imagination into reality. We begin with a spark of inspiration and build that in to a mastery of light, color, and texture. At the heart of creation lies the ultimate in design and layout. We need only to allow our creative impressions to surface and unfold on the canvas that is our event.

One of the biggest mistakes one encounters when programming an event or show is the tendency to over program. It is easy to get caught up in a whirlwind of creation and imagination. Focus and clarity are what are needed at this moment. It is also important to build your looks with the event in mind and not just what one thinks looks cool.

When programming, take into account all of the ingredients that brought you to the show. This will allow you to remember not only why you came, but also why others came who are attending the event. With that knowledge you can create programming that is appropriate to the situation, and your lighting cues will have the proper impact intended by those who hired you.

STEVE LIEBERMAN, DESIGNER AND PROGRAMMER

Programming moving lights can be a somewhat daunting and often challenging task. That being said, it is important to start your programming session with an understanding of what you aim to accomplish. You should always have your laptop with you! Keep copies of the latest software for your console as well as previous versions. It is also important to save your show to your hard drive, not just floppy disks. This is probably the most important part of programming!

There are several ways to achieve the same results. My best advice would be to learn the long way first so that you have an understanding of the syntax. Do not be afraid of your console. As long as you save often, you should be willing to hit every button. If you don't know what a button does, ask. If you encounter a bug in the software, report it. This helps all of us. When there is an opportunity to sit next to another programmer while they're working, do it. You'll probably learn something you didn't know before. Always be willing to help others.

STEVE OWENS, DESIGNER

When you start your programming, you may or may not have a concept of what it is that you want to see. There is a formula that I follow. A start point (setting up of your console) — this is what I find to be the hardest part. Setting up your groups, colors, beams, and preset focuses. I'll do a basic block format on the board. Then as I am programming each song I will add to my palettes, such as new focus positions and new colors, etc. I try not to be repetitive, meaning not to see the same things over and over. Start off with a WOW. Then settle in to a groove for a while and start building and building. So then you're heightening their senses without anyone knowing it. Then throw in the hammer, kill 'em. Throw the whole nine yards at them. Something to leave them in awe and still wanting more.

SUSAN ROSE, PROGRAMMER

Try to work with every type of moving light that you have the opportunity to do so. Don't be afraid to experiment with all of the parameters. You can come up with some really cool stuff by accident sometimes. But if you really know what the particular moving light is capable of, you can come up with specific looks much more easily. Always keep learning new consoles, and always keep learning more about the consoles that you regularly program on.

TIM GRIVAS, PROGRAMMER

If you are a creative person, then you're lucky. Creativity is not something you can learn. Download as much technical details into your brain as you can so you will not rely on technical expertise to make your creative ideas come true, be unstoppable. The Automated Lighting Programmer of today should know video as well as well as lighting.

TIMOTHY F. ROGERS, PROGRAMMER

The three most important qualities that a good programmer needs to have are:

1. The ability to communicate well with others. Communication is one of the most important jobs of a good programmer.
2. Having a great eye. For example, the ability to blend the automated system with the conventional system, to know what color or image fits the mood or feeling on stage. To be a good second set of eyes for the designer is wonderful help during the design process of a show.
3. Speed. Speed is of the essence while programming a show. The last thing that the designer wants is to have to wait for his or her programmer to complete a task. If the task at hand is going to take some time, just explain that to the designer or the director (communication) and if time allows, complete the task. Knowing your desk and being able to think about what you have done and what you are about to do as well as what might be coming up are all important elements to speed.

VICKIE CLAIBORNE, PROGRAMMER

A successful programmer walks a fine line between lighting designer and button pusher. Every designer will have their own style and personality, and not all will want to get input from the programmer. Get to know the LD before expressing and asserting your opinions. Then if he or she seems receptive to your influence, gently offer up your ideas. This will build the LD's confidence in you, thereby possibly ensuring that they will call you again for their next show because you made them look great and you were accommodating to them on their terms.

Appendix

Sydney 2000 Olympic Games Journal

Figure A.1 A Bold Lighting Look During the Sydney 2000 Olympic Games Opening Ceremony

The 2000 Summer Olympics held in Sydney Australia was a magnificent time for many of the greatest athletes of the world to gather and compete. As with most modern Olympic games extravagant productions marked the opening and closing of the games. Because the show took place in a giant sporting arena and would be seen by more than 4 billion people live via television, every bit of the production was large scale. In fact even the venue was built to serve two main purposes: the athletic events and the opening and closing ceremonies. I was honored to be part of the lighting team for these worldwide spectacles. There were far too many people involved in the production for me to list them all here, however Table A.1 lists those directly involved in the programming of the automated lighting.

The tremendous effort put forth to make these productions successful can only be credited to everyone on the team. I think this show was one of the largest collaborative efforts of lighting programmers to date. I felt it would be beneficial to myself and our industry to notate our experiences as they happened.

What follows is my daily journal that I diligently kept while working on the shows. Usually returning to my temporary home early in the morning after programming all night long, I would spend 10–15 minutes writing out the events of the day.

Table A.1   The Automated Lighting Programming Team

John Rayment	Lighting Designer	
Rohan Thorton	Lighting Director	
Trudy Daegleish	Associate Lighting Designer	
Jo Elliot	Assistant Lighting Designer	
Dave Wilkinson	Jo's Assistant	
Robert Bell	Wholehog II pogrammer & WYSIWYG Specialist	On field Cyberlights
Ian "Gooche" Blackburn	Wholehog II programmer	One quarter of the main field fixtures (Closing Ceremony)
Vickie Claiborne	Wholehog II programmer	One quarter of the main field fixtures and conventionals
Jason Fripp	Wholehog II programmer	One quarter of the main field fixtures
Mark Hammer	Wholehog II programmer	Stage fixtures
Rohan Harrison	Wholehog II programmer	One quarter of the main field fixtures
Megan McGahan	Strand 550i Programmer	Audience lighting
Jason McKinnon	Wholehog II programmer	Rooftop Space Cannons
Dean Price	Wholehog II programmer/ Space Cannon Technician	Field Space Cannons
Brad Schiller	Wholehog II programmer	One quarter of the main field fixtures and conventionals
Brendon West	Wholehog II programmer	Field Space Cannons

Figure A.2   Brad Schiller at His Console Prior to the Sydney 2000 Olympic Games Closing Ceremonies

BRAD SCHILLER'S OLYMPIC JOURNAL

Day 1, August 21, 2000

Today was the first day. We started out at Spectak Productions. In a small room we had 7 Wholehog IIs and 7 WYSIWYG computers each with a vision 2000 (see Figure A.3). Each of these computers were hooked up on a network as well. There are 21 monitors to support all this gear. We spent part of the morning hooking up monitors and getting things in place. We then talked with John Rayment (LD) about some of his plans and goals for the show.

I cleared all the desks, added the current software and merged in the patch from previous test disks. We all then set to the task of building groups as defined by John. Once the groups were built, then we had to discuss how he plans to call the fixtures. There are numbers everyplace (DMX, tech numbers, LD numbers, console numbers, etc.). We decided to number things the way the LD was used to them and we had to rename our groups to match this. Jo (assistant LD) kept bringing us paperwork with various numbers and charts and we kept updating and building groups, all the while making sure we were each building the same things. We also built seven simple color palettes to match the colors in the scrollers. (Figure A.3)

While the four main consoles were busy with this, Dean was busy building his own groups, palettes and effects with the Space Cannons. Robert Bell was continually updating the WYSIWYG file via the network. His console will control the 20 Cyberlight fixtures on the set pieces, so he was concentrating on the WYSIWYG and not worrying about his Hog show. Mark's desk has Studio Colors and conventionals on it (set lighting) and he spent the day building his groups and palettes (and updating and correcting the WYSIWYG file with Robert).

After lunch we started the task of positions. Everything in the show is based on a huge grid laid out over the field. The grid is 29×47 squares. We have to make position palettes for about 1/3 of these. The plan is to use Auto Focus in WYSIWYG, but there is a hardware problem with the MIDI cards, so this is delayed until tomorrow. In the mean time, we had to discuss the best way to organize all these positions so when the LD calls out position F-20 we can quickly find it. Since we did not have the auto focus working we started out making the palettes by hand. This gave us plenty of time to figure out the best way to organize the palettes. We decided to use the page up and down keys to make a page for each letter of the alphabet (plus the three double letters) and have all the positive and negative number positions for that letter on each page. We are even going

Figure A.3 Consoles and WYSIWYG Computers Setup at Spectak Productions

to try to make macros to jump directly to each letter so that we can speed up the palette selection process. It would make sense to just give each position a unique number and key them in, but since the entire production from sets to choreography to lighting use the same grid system we have to maintain consistency.

At the end of the day we all had completed one line (the center "O" line) consisting of 23 palettes. Robert Bell was going to stay late to try to fix the WYSIWYG problem. For disk saving we decided to run on a three disk leapfrog method. At the end of each day I archived each final day show disk to my laptop. We also switched to new disks at least once a week to ensure good disks. Tomorrow we are planning to start by viewing the video of rehearsals and then finishing the positions. Once those are done we will start on the cuing (which John calls "plotting").

Day 2, August 22, 2000

Today we started by viewing the videos of the opening and closing ceremonies. These were videos that were made by the Olympic committee to present the concepts of the shows. All I can say is WOW! This is going to be a huge spectacular. There are some amazing things that are going to happen.

Today we started by updating the 145 positions we each have. We used the Auto Focus feature of WYSIWYG, which made a huge difference. We would click on each point in the grid and then just record the position. This was so much easier than moving each fixture one at a time. Of course, when we get to the arena we will have to update each and every fixture in each and every position. We decided to use the "page down" method for each letter of the alphabet and this seems to work well. I built 30 macros to assist in jumping to each letter. We then merged these macros into each of the other three consoles. After this was completed, we all built stage focus positions. This was challenging, as we had to adjust the height for each of the four stages in WYSIWYG as we went along.

Next John Rayment came in and described some looks he wanted. We had to build the fence wash. This is a straight down focus around the edge of the track. Next we had to do a "horse wash," which is a crossed focus on the fence line. This sounds simple, but for the west side we have two programmers that have to coordinate their cross focus so that the end result is a symmetrical focus. Next the east side desks have to make their focus match the west side. The problem becomes deciding the best way to do the cross focus. At first all four of us set out with our own processes for the focus. We quickly found out that we each were doing a different method. We had to stop and determine the best way to do this and then all build the focus. Using the WYSIWYG we each turned on a view to enable us to see our east or west partner.

Vickie and I brainstormed about the closing ceremony. There is no rehearsal for the show. We will have to "wing it" for most of the show. We are planning to propose to John to build 30 or so "on the fly" looks and chases that are the same on each desk. This way he can call for the random color chase on the main stage and then all of us will have the same effect. We will see what he thinks. Tomorrow we are going to the stadium to test our shows and see that everything is working correctly. Then the next 5 days or so we will be building the cues.

Day 3, August 23, 2000

We started out the day back at the Spectak office where we first watched some videos of the rehearsals and an animation of the horses. After that we began to build what are called "patterns." These are focus positions that form a certain pattern. We first defined four sections to start with … all in the form of the Olympic Rings. We now have the "Arrivals" rings and the "Arrivals" pools. We also have the "Horses" rings and the "Horses" pools. We were very careful along the way to decide on the name of each position and make sure we all refer to it with the same label. Next we had to figure out how to build what the LD is looking for. This was straightforward for the pools, but the rings proved to be a challenge. How do you split 4 desks across 5 rings knowing that later you do not know which lights will be used for which portion of which ring? We all brainstormed on this trying to decide the best approach. We finally decided to try an idea from Jason. We each divided our lights into groups of ten and built each ring 6 (or 7 depending on the desk) times. This way we can use some or all of our lights to form any part of any ring. We then each set out to build all these positions. With 70 fixtures and 10 positions on each ring this took some time. Jason and Rohan used the WYSIWYG method. That is, they used Auto Focus to click on their screen each position and then record this to the desk. Vickie and I decided to do it the old fashioned console method and just dialed all our lights into position. When we completed these tasks, then we all packed up and went to the stadium.

We arrived at the stadium and went to see our home … WOW, we will be sitting just below the mega-VIP seating (royalty, presidents, etc.) and are in the prime spot in the very center. We then loaded up our shows and started to play with the lights. As we predicted the positions were close but not exact due to differences in fixtures versus WYSIWYG. We all then started playing when we noticed a problem. We have a steppy DMX problem. When the lights are moving slowly then appear steppy. We do not know if the problem is a Hog problem or a problem with the Strand ethernet network. The crew is going to test this by running a line directly to a console and see what happens. The problem is not seen in the WYSI-WYG (even on the network) so we suspect the problem is in the boxes that convert the Ethernet back to DMX. After that we all went to a pub right next to the stadium and had some good beer.

Day 4, August 24, 2000

We started the day by building the focuses for the "Horse" rings. John had precharted which fixtures went to which rings by groups of ten. We then set out to combine our groups to make the circle. Usually it was three programmers to make the ring. It took a few minutes, but Rohan soon figured out a good method. He suggested that we each divide our ten lights and place the furthest two on a tangent to the circle and then fill in the gap evenly. This worked well and in no time we had five perfect ring focuses build by combining four desks!

Next it was time to start plotting (cuing). John came in and we all built cue 1. It was a big moment! ☺ As we continued building the cues we would all talk about how to build the needed effect and then each build it in the same manner. We also moved very carefully to make sure everyone was on the same cue. Mark was not there today (and will not be for several days), also Dean was not there. Robert took over on Dean's console and I programmed Mark's and mine. It was a little confusing at first until I got around his groups and built some of my own. Eventually Robert had to stay at Dean's desk so for a while I was programming cues on three desks at one time! Sometimes, Vickie would lean over to my desk and build the cue if I was busy on the others. It will probably stay this way for the next few days.

This morning while building some of the first cues, the solution to the steppy Cybers we saw at the stadium the night before came to me. I remembered that the fixture library we are using has a bug with the Mspeed channel. The default was set for the fastest Mspeed and not

Xfade. This is why we saw the jittery beams. I then realized it all clicked and all the symptoms pointed to this as the cause. The fix is very simple (change the default). I told John what I thought of and he immediately called the crew at the stadium. They agreed that this looked like this could be the solution. Tonight they tried it and I was correct . . . the problem is solved! Next we found a problem with the Mspeed chart for Cyberlight. I have confirmed (using Status Cue software) that the Mspeed chart used for Cybers is NOT the same as other High End Systems (HES) fixtures. When I finish writing this, Vickie and I will build the new chart into the Hog library. Vickie will bring up the values in Status Cue, view them as both label and DMX, then tell me and I will enter them into the library. In the morning I will rebuild all the shows with the new correct Mspeed library. Wow, we have had fun with Mspeed.

Day 5, August 25, 2000

Today I started by trying to load my new library for the Cybers. For some reason there was a bug that was ignoring the invert for the color channels. This was really annoying me as I did not even change the color mix channels, but the Hog was inverting them. It took an hour off the morning, but I finally figured out how to fix this. Once I managed to merge in the correct library I realized that this would cause all the position focuses to scrunch up one after the other. This would destroy the nice charting we made of the 145 positions. So we skipped all this and started plotting (cuing). We built a really cool chase that was building the 5 Olympic rings as the horses ran through them. This required a coordinated effort of 30 cues between the 4 desks. This took some time, but we got it worked out so that we can make the cue work. After lunch I was charting Mspeed trying to make a conversion from the incorrect chart to the correct chart to avoid the merging. Vickie suggested making palettes of the common Mspeed values. We built the palettes based on what the Mspeed should be and assigning it to the equivalent incorrect Mspeed chart in the library we are using. We continued building cues and I was still programming on two desks. At the end of the day we had all built about 100 total cues and made it about 2/5th through the show. Tomorrow (Saturday) is a day off and Vickie and I plan to go with Henry and Victory to experience the Sydney Harbor Bridge climb. For a small fee we will get to climb to the top of one of the most famous bridges in the world and enjoy a splendid view of Sydney Harbor. John is going to a rehearsal. After this we will not get a day off again for 3 weeks until after the show is over! The show is 3 weeks from tonight.

Day 6, August 26, 2000

This was a day off. Vickie and I went to the bridge climb on our own. No one else wanted to go (chickens!). It was a lot of fun. They have planned it very well and thought of everything. We did a night climb, which was fun, but I would suggest a day climb as the photos are better.

Day 7, August 27, 2000

We started off the day with John telling us his plans for how far we should get today. All seven programmers were here today so we all could work just on our own desks. We started building simple cues, and then we hit another huge sequence. For the "Fire" section we had to have all the lights move from the north to the south of the field. They had to move in a 40-meter wide chunk. It had to look as if this "chunk" was moving down the field. This sounds simple until you think about fading in and out lights five at a time and doing this across four desks. Everyone started trying to figure out the best way to do this and we were getting no place. Finally I got out a piece of paper and charted it out. It ended up taking 20 cues each with various groups of lights fading in and out. I then called out all the lights for each cue and whoever had them on their desk would enter the correct information. Once we finished this, then we had to apply the timing John wanted (40 seconds to center and 1 minute from there to the end). Finally we could run the cue. This minute and half cue took about 45 minutes to write. We are all learning the best methods for programming on multiple desks. Thank goodness that John is calm and has the ability to look at the big picture. This means he has to look at seven WYSIWYG screens at one time and envision what the real cue will look like. We can turn multiple (or all) lights on one WYSIWYG, but this just gets really busy on the screen with too many lines. (Figure A.4)

We then continued onward plotting more cues. John would call out groups of lights and their positions on the grid. We would each use our macros to jump to the correct letter (section of the grid) and choose the exact coordinate. This method seems to work great and speed up finding positions. Late in the day we also built a combined color look where we

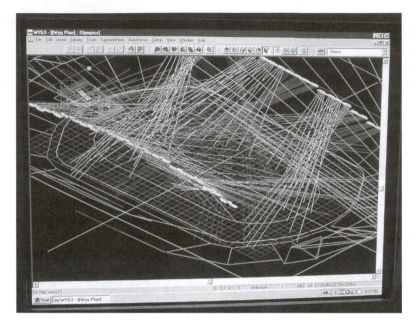

Figure A.4 A WYSIWYG Screen Displaying Output from All Consoles

each used four colors across four pools on the field. John then said that on each side of the field he wanted alternating colors from each programmer and then the inverse from the other side of the field.

Two ideas I had to make large group programming sessions easier in the future is to: (a) have a sign like the post office (now serving #) and use as now building cue number and (b) have a large wipe board in the room for charting out these large coordinated efforts.

Day 8, August 28, 2000

Another day of WYSIWYG. We are now over 180 cues and just about to the athletes' entrance. Today we all had the same feeling . . . we are ready to get onto the real rig. This much WYSIWYGing with just sections of the rig really removes us from the big picture. The renderings we do every night of the entire rig help. However, it is still hard to watch the rehearsal videos and realize that it is the same big show we are lighting. On Wednesday we move into the stadium and it should all come together for us then.

We built some other big coordinated cues and have found an important key ... we write down exactly what John says he is looking for and then we brainstorm. This way there is no confusion later as to what he wants. John also seems to now see that he has to think about the time it takes to build a coordinated cue (all lights fade up from center to out) versus the end result for the show. Many times it may be better to not take the time to build a huge cue that may be too subtle for the audience or TV.

Day 9, August 29, 2000

Today was the last day at Spectak working with just WYSIWYG. We started the morning building cues. We all charted and made the map of Australia by combining all desks. This cue looks really cool when you see the lights form the outline. Next Compaq came in and did a big photo shoot that took too long. They are supplying the computers and monitors we use for WYSIWYG. After lunch we built more cues and had several other coordinated cues. These went much better as we all have the routine down now. We then went though all our cues and noted which focuses we are using. Of the 145 original positions on the grid we are each using about 33–35. We also have each created an additional 70 custom positions. Since we have charted this, we will only update the focuses we used. When we start programming in the stadium, we will still have the WYSIWYG hooked up. We can then see if when we use a palette that we have not updated on the real rig yet (it will be off in WYSIWYG, but not the real lights). The next two nights we will be updating positions and then start in with rehearsals.

Day 10, August 30, 2000

Well, we started in the stadium tonight. It was quite a site to see all seven desks lined up in the center of the audience! We set off updating our positions. We sent Dave down to the field to mark the positions with cones (witches hats). We then started to focus the positions that we actually used in cues. The plan was to have each person do each position so that we would not put too much light on the field. This did not go well as some people did not like waiting, so we started doing multiple positions at a time. This worked okay except that it was not completely dark on the field. There were sports lights on for the crew putting down the flooring and working on the stage. This became a problem for me as I have 30 of my lights on the extreme ends of the truss. With the throw distance they are very difficult to see. Since I am on the opposite side of the field, my lights are harder to see than those on the same side as us. Rohan has his fixtures on the other side too, but they are all near center. I became somewhat frustrated because some of the programmers were not respecting the darkness needed for me to see my fixtures. I had to repeatedly ask them to not work on washes, audience lights, etc. Their lights had no dim problems and they did not understand. I just put on my headphones and tried to get over it. Hopefully tomorrow we will get some dark time. Plus, right now the real floor is not down and Dave is measuring the positions. I am sure that we will have to update them all again (and again). We have a great vantage point for the show (dead center), but with all our monitors it is kind of cramped. We are supposed to get some flat screens in and that should help. Oh yea, we also discovered that WYSIWYG had the zoom backwards so we had to invert the zoom data in all our cues.

Day 11, August 31, 2000

Second night in the stadium. Tonight was pretty much the same as last night. Jo and Dave had worked out a good system for placing the cones and this helped. They had part of the flooring down (carpet actually), but it was placed the wrong way around. Dave got a little confused at one point where it measured differently than the floor was marked. We will have to wait until the floor is down to really know for sure if everything is correct. I ran through my cues and WOW it looks good. When focusing one light at a time I was losing site of the big picture. I really was not seeing great levels of light; however, once I ran the cues and saw the pools form, etc. I could really see the big picture. The production is so huge that we are running into other problems too … that is we have not had dark time yet because there are others working on the stage and the floor. Also, the lighting techs are shutting down our fixtures and leaving at 2 A.M. so we have to stop. We have asked to have techs waiting until we are done so that we can work longer. Tomorrow (Friday) is our last day off until after the show. We start again on Saturday with rehearsals. Tonight we also finally got to see the cauldron light and rise up the stadium. This is going to be a really cool moment when it happens. It is supposed to be a big surprise, but I just saw shots on TV from last night's rehearsal. They even mentioned the "laser lights" referring to the Space Cannons. Oh yea … also I spoke with Megan and told her about the lamp strobing and boosting on the Studio Beams. She then put all 250 fixtures in the lamp strobing and it was great!

Day 12, September 1, 2000

This was our last day off until after the show. We start tomorrow working for 14 nights straight. We got a VIP tech tour of the Sydney Opera House.

Day 13, September 2, 2000

Today was the first day of rehearsals. Also, it marked the first time we arrived since lockdown had started. We had to go through security to get in. It was still daylight when we arrived (5 P.M.) so we went and had dinner. Then we started working with our fixtures trying to run some cues while the performers were rehearsing "Nature" and "Tin." We had the entire rig and the sports lights were off. However, the Halide Metal Inert gas (HMIs) still had no scrollers on them so now we had our own white light to fight. We parked the HMIs at 0, but then the techs told us that there is a heat shield problem and that we have to leave the shutters open. So now we had to leave all our HMIs open and in white on the field. This made it very frustrating for everyone as we really could not do any work. Finally when rehearsal was over, we were able to power down the HMIs and we could finally have dark time. This was the first time that we had dark time in the stadium. We all started checking positions, etc. Also, Dean finally had all his space cannons working and was able to update his focuses too. So again we all had to share the darkness and respect what the others were doing so that we could all see. We had Jo and Dave lay out cones for the "Horse" rings and we all touched up those positions. We then ran the cues (Dean blacked out for us) and they looked GREAT! It was super to see all four desks form the Olympic Rings and then morph into pools.

On the way back to the bus we hopped a ride in the back of a police paddy wagon! We all climbed in the cage and the door was locked shut.

Day 14, September 3, 2000

What a wasted day. We had to show up at 4 P.M. today for the techs. The sun was out so we did not do anything until later. Once it was dark out we could do things, except that it was protocol rehearsal. This is lit in solid white light and takes a long time. This includes the volunteers and the athletes' parade. So we sat there doing nothing most of the night. Once we got to a point that we had to do something, the Strand network failed and we all had no signal to our lights. It turned out that a UPS was unplugged and we were running all day on the UPS, but it finally died. At about midnight we finally had dark time again and we were able to finish our positions. Jo and Dave mapped out the "Arrival" rings and we all placed all our lights on each of the rings. We also touched up some other focuses. Dean went down to the field to program the Space Cannons. The HMIs will not be ready with their scrollers until Tuesday, so on Monday we will not do much either. Then we will start on Tuesday with late nights plotting cues.

Day 15, September 4, 2000

Tonight we rehearsed "Nature" and they did it in full costume. It was nice to see the show start to come together. We ran our cues, but we dimmed out the HMIs as we did not have the scrollers. Dean had about half his Space Cannons working and was doing the color washes on the field. John had a camera and a monitor so he could check how it will look on camera. Dean had a great amber wash on the floor that looked great to the eye, but was really dull on camera. When asked if he could make them redder, he said the amber was as close to red as they can get. This will mean that we may have to alter some cues to try to compensate. We stopped early to let the crew work on the HMIs. We watched a full rehearsal of the cauldron and this was incredible. Tomorrow we start working from 6 P.M. till 5 A.M. and hopefully will get everything to work and are able to work on our cues. Megan has started adding in cues for the audience lights (she now has about eight).

Day 16, September 5, 2000

Tonight they rehearsed part of "Tin" and then "Arrivals." "Arrivals" is the section where the people form a giant map of Australia and then 2000 children run into the map. It was great that once the people formed the map (before the kids ran in), the director stopped them and made them stand in place while we focused all 300 Cybers on them. After "Arrivals" they rehearsed the athletes' entrance again. This took about an hour and we all just took a break. After that the field was ours. The director of

Figure A.5   The Number titled "Nature" as It Appeared During the Show

"Tin" came up and sat with John and we all plotted cues. When we would build a look then John would say "feed the machine cue 160." We finally had all the scrollers working today although each one could crash at any time and this is somewhat worrisome. Dean reverted back to a crew person to get all the Procon gear working and Brendon took over programming the Space Cannons. We had to stop at 2:30 A.M. because the bomb sweep was going on. Tomorrow we are starting the long hours. The stage crew had to rip up the flooring and pull all the plywood they put down as it was becoming a real mess.

Day 17, September 6, 2000

Tonight we rehearsed "Deep Sea Dreaming." This number is very amazing. There are fish flying all over the place. We also watched the horses rehearse. After the cast left we sat and programmed the end of the show (speeches, etc.) and watched the cauldron again. We are all running into a few problems where we will alter a cue and we must think ahead to the next cue and not destroy our tracking. Each of us have run into situations where we edit one cue and then find we have ruined another by changing a focus in the first cue that tracked into the next cue. To prevent this we are trying to remember to load state and update cues before altering prior cues. Jo and Rohan Thorton went up in a helicopter to check the Space Cannon and audience cues from that camera point of view. There are still many problems with the HMIs and scrollers. Hopefully this will get worked out soon.

Day 18, September 7, 2000

We rehearsed the end of "Eternity" tonight, which is when most of the cast from all the sections comes out on the field. This was the first time they ever assembled everybody and they spent time learning new choreography. After that the horses rehearsed again. We adjusted and rehearsed our cues. After rehearsals we plotted cues for the torch entries and the cauldron. We then all left and let Brendon have some time to get his positions built. We still have HMI and scroller problems.

Day 19, September 8, 2000

We saw "Awakenings" for the first time. This section has a large Aboriginal cast. They rehearsed part of their number, but I do not think they rehearsed all of it. Next we rehearsed with the horses again. We had to modify our horse rings to the actual rings they were making. John rebuilt the first few cues several times before landing on the HMIs during the horses' entrance and the Space Cannons for their exits. Next we ran through most of the cues and made adjustments from John's notes. Tomorrow is the first dress rehearsal with an audience of 110,000. It will be the first time the show has been run in order in its entirety (except the cauldron). The scrollers and HMIs still were not all working, but TV likes the splotchy white areas, so now we will have to build in some of the "messed up" looks that we have had due to equipment problems.

Day 20, September 9, 2000

We had the first ever run through of the entire show and in front of 110,000 people! Lighting wise we had no train wrecks or major problems. John has his work cut out for him on getting the lighting correct for TV. Often during the rehearsal he was trying to add more light and the TV people kept trying to adjust. They ended up just fighting each other. At the end of the night they had a big meeting and worked everything out.

Day 21, September 10, 2000

Tonight was another first ... we had the stadium all to ourselves to work on cuing. There were no other rehearsals and we had a great night of plotting. John had several of the directors come up and we rebuilt the cues for those sections. We had one camera on the monitor so we could watch the levels. Everyone really liked our horse ring cue last night, except that it was not bright enough for television. They want to do an aerial shot as we build the rings as the horses form them. We had originally built this 30 part cue using 10 lights from each console in each ring. We decided to rebuild these cues and use 40 lights from each console per ring. We also decided to only use the lights closest to the ring. So Rohan and I had 3 rings and Vickie and Jason have 2 rings. Also, Rohan and I tried to make them so that the dimmer lights (without narrow lenses) are closer than those with narrow lenses. This made mine somewhat difficult as I had fixtures in a wacky order. The rings read very well now on the camera and we all feel really good about this (now) 40 part cue. Tomorrow we will start again with rehearsals of some sections and rebuilding of some cues for "Arrivals" and "Eternity."

Day 22, September 11, 2000

We started the night watching while the band rehearsed their entrance and exit. This sounds quick and easy, but with a marching band of 2500 it is no easy task. During the wait, Vickie and I got to hold a real Olympic torch. It was not heavy as we had been told. After that we rehearsed the horses again. This time all 400 were wearing in-ear monitors so it made it difficult to know what they were doing etc. Our new improved horse rings look great. The problem now is that the horses do not form the same rings every time. Because the TV crew plans to do an over head shot (which looks great) we are going to get our rings looking great and let the horses look like they did not form them correctly. We also watched the cauldron again and the TV crew rehearsed their shots. This is going to look super on television and in-person. After the horses, we plotted more cues and started some cleaning up of cues. Tomorrow we will do a technical rehearsal and go through all the cues and do "housekeeping."

Figure A.6 The Number titled "Fire" as It Appeared During the Show

Day 23, September 12, 2000

Tonight was a technical rehearsal that went on till about 1:30 A.M. when it stopped due to technical errors. We actually saw some new flying elements for "Tin" that we had never seen. We also found out that our horse ring cue has been cut. All the work we did is now gone. Oh well, maybe it will get added back in. After the rehearsal ended, we all plotted cues for several more hours. John is having a tough time with various directors, television people, artistic directors, etc. all giving their input to how they think the lighting should be. We are continually making changes to most of our cues and trying to keep up with all the tracking information. Tomorrow is another dress rehearsal and we are all looking forward to it.

Day 24, September 13, 2000

Tonight's dress rehearsal in front of 110,000 went very well. Everything ran extremely smooth up until "Eternity." This section needs a lot of work in all areas, not just lighting. TV liked most of the show and we just need to balance some of the images to get rid of hot spots, etc. Rohan Thorton has been very good about filling us in on all the politics currently going on. The television director will say the segment looks great, but he wants to light the people exiting each segment so he wants us to hold the lighting looks longer. The segment director will want to relight the entire number with new colors, pools, etc. The artistic director wants to get the transitions happening sooner so that we do not see the people exiting. Each of these people come to John and voice their opinion. He has to try to figure out how to please everyone (and himself). If he makes the changes for the segment director, then the television director complains and vice versa. Rohan has asked that we all try to make "commonsense" decisions on our own and modify looks that we feel should be modified. This is a usual thing for programmers to do and most LDs just never know it happens or take it for granted. This is fairly easy for half the programmers, but the four of us with the bulk of the Cybers have to act as one. If one of us changes our Cybers to 60% then it looks funny if the other 3 desks are at 100%. So we all just talk and decide what will be best.

After rehearsal we did a cue by cue run through to do "housekeeping" on all our cues, setups, etc. We worked until 5 A.M. John had left to light a building downtown, so Jo called us through the cues and gave us John's notes. Tomorrow we will go through all the cues again with John and Rohan and modify all levels for television.

Day 25, September 14, 2000

Tonight we worked until 6 A.M. cleaning up cues and rebuilding "Awakenings" and "Eternity." We had to stop working for more than 2 hours while they rehearsed with the torchbearers. Their identity is supposed to be kept secret so we had to leave it dark during the entire time. We all feel that we have a fantastic show and are ready to run the show tomorrow.

Day 26, September 15, 2000

WOW, what a super show! We all had a great time and everything worked perfectly. We made a few live adjustments and that added to the fun. We were able to watch the TV show on a monitor in front of us while watching the real show at the same time. It looked super! Even the segments and cues that we rebuilt at 4 A.M. the night before looked incredible. The crowd enjoyed the show and seeing 110,000 people wave their flashlights in the stands was awesome. Vickie and I cheered on the U.S. team as they entered and then we all cheered for Australia. Then it was time for the lighting of the cauldron. This was going great until the trolley got stuck and the cauldron did not move. This was a very scary moment for all of us to see this huge moment almost not work. After what seemed like forever (actually was about 3 minutes) the cauldron made its way to the top. The crowd still loved it and every one was thrilled. After the show we all partied until after 6 A.M. We were told that during the show designer Patrick Woodroff called and said this was the best light show he had ever seen!

<TIME OFF DURING THE OLYMPIC GAMES>

Day 40, September 29, 2000

Tonight we went back to the stadium to begin working on the "Closing." The crew was in last night to check the rig. Everything was

Figure A.7   The Number titled "Tin" as It Appeared During the Show

working well. Vickie has flown back to the States and now Gooch is programming her desk, also Robert Bell has gone home. We first sat down with John and discussed his plans for the show. We then formulated the best way to lay this out on the consoles. We decided to set it up much like a rock show and make different pages for each song or segment of the closing. This way we can have bumps, chases, etc. specific to that song. We will each have a master cuelist on a template page and then add in the other cues via the separate pages. Gooch and I also have two faders for HMIs on the template page. In addition, we have to be ready to throw in anything that John calls out. Basically tonight we roughed in some positions with the sports lights still on. Tomorrow we will have it darker, but still not complete darkness. Then on Sunday we see a daytime rehearsal and then run the show for the world that night. There is very little setup or rehearsal time. One good thing is that we will get in ear monitors of the music so we can do things on the beat. Things went well until they turned the power off on us at 4:30 A.M.

Day 41, September 30, 2000

When I walked into the stadium they were playing the U.S. National Anthem. It was a medal ceremony and the United States had won gold. This was great to walk in and cheer on our winners, and they were just down in front of me too. We started working sometime after midnight and worked through the night till almost 6 A.M. We never had any dark time as they were building the stage and had sports lights up all night long. We managed to plot cues for about half the songs. We also prepared "wing it" masters and palettes for the rest of the show. John has notes on what he wants to do, we just do not have cues for it. Tomorrow we have a rehearsal in the daytime and then the show starts. We plan to update positions on the stages during the preshow as this will be the first dark time we have with the stages in place. One interesting thing is that this is the type of show that it is easy for a programmer to just wing it, but since the rig is spread across eight consoles this is now difficult. If I decide to throw in a random strobe at a point in a song and no one else does, then my lights look like they are doing the wrong thing. So we all just have to count on John to call what he wants and that is what we will do. We went home, had about 4 hours sleep, and now go back for the rehearsal and show.

Day 42, October 1, 2000

We went in at noon and the stage was still not built. During the day they built the stage and we sat around. We never actually rehearsed anything. Doors were at 4 P.M., but they held them till about 4:30. Even then, they were still building the stage. Around 6 P.M. the marathon runners came in, and then at 7:30 was the preshow. This was our *only* time to update positions. The show started at 8 P.M. We all turned on "live programmer" and off we went. We had preprogrammed about half the songs in the show and the rest we just made up as we went along. During the show John would call "stand by for all Cybers on stage in blue from east and magenta from west . . . Go." We all also improvised during most of the songs using the "wing it" stuff we had premade. The show looked great and John was very happy. He was thrilled that many times we all just took over and made the show happen and then he would call just the major changes, etc. Mark Hammer did a super job with the fixtures on the stage and we all had a great time.

Figure A.8   A Moment from the Closing Ceremony

Table A.2 Sydney 2000 Olympic Games Lighting Equipment

3,288,960	Watts
111,169	Meters of Cable
64,775	Meters of Power Cable
52,260	Man Hours
46,394	Meters of Data Cable
14,208	Channels of DMX
13,704	Amps Single Phase
7054	Cables
4568	Amps Three Phase
4535	Power Cables
2519	Data Cables
1628	Total Fixtures
970	Automated Fixtures
658	Analog Fixtures
541	Meters of Truss
300	HES Cyberlight Turbo
207	Racks of Power Distribution/Dimming
200	De Sisti Ducci
136	HES Studio Beam
132	HES Studio Color
112	ACL
111	Kilometers of Cable
106	Lighting Crew
100	4 kW HMI
99	Tons of Equipment
92	Kino Flow
90	Rigging Points
78	Chain Motor
76	DMX Splitter
60	Par 64
57	Mains Connection
48	7k Space Cannon Ireos Pro
40	HES Cyberlight
35	Streams of DMX
34	Tons of Cable
28	Space Cannon Easy 2000
22	40 Foot Trailers of Equipment
18	2k Lycian Followspot
14	Wholehog II
11	Weeks On-Site
8	4k Space Cannon Ireos Pro
8	4k Lycian Followspot
4	Lighting Suppliers
2	Strand 550i
1	Opening Ceremony
1	Closing Ceremony

Glossary

8-Bit DMX   A parameter that uses a single DMX channel for control.

16-Bit DMX   A parameter that uses two DMX channels for control. Usually used with pan and tilt for finer resolution of control.

Automated Light   A remotely controlled lighting fixture, usually with the ability to move and/or change colors.

Ballyhoo   A programmed move of automated lighting fixtures where the lights are seen to move randomly within a defined area.

Bank   *See* Page.

Beamage   A term used to describe beams of light projected from lighting fixtures as seen in the air.

Board   *See* Console.

Bump   To change the value of a parameter at a time of 0. Usually assigned to a momentary button on the lighting console.

Bump Button   A button on a lighting console that creates an action when pressed and another action when released.

Chase   A looping set of cues.

Console   A custom developed input control device used for programming lighting.

Conventional Light   A nonautomated lighting fixture, usually working in conjunction with dimmers.

Crossfade   A timing value assigned to fixture parameters used to control the duration of a change from one DMX value to another.

Cue   The basic placeholder in a lighting console for all programming data. Often also referred to as step or look.

Cuelist   A series of cues intended to play back in a particular order. Also referred to as sequence or stack.

Desk   *See* Console.

Dimmer   A device used to control the intensity of incandescent lighting fixtures.

DMX   Digital multiplexing, a programming protocol commonly used by lighting products. The protocol consists of 512 channels each with 256 values. Generally a single channel controls one function of an automated lighting fixture.

DMX Address   The starting DMX channel used by a lighting fixture or dimmer.

DMX Universe   A DMX Universe contains 512 channels of control. Often referred to as a world or output.

Effects   Mathematical calculations used by a lighting console or fixture to create premade chases.

Ethernet   A protocol for delivering data between devices. DMX is often converted to an Ethernet protocol to allow for data distribution.

Fader   A device on a lighting console to allow for manual crossfades of parameters.

Fixture   A lighting instrument.

Fixture Number   The number used by a lighting programmer to access a particular fixture during programming, usually different than the DMX address of the fixture.

Flyout   A programmed move of automated lighting fixtures where the lights are seen to move vertically from one position to another. For example, a typical Flyout cue moves fixtures from the stage to above the audience.

FOH   Front of house, the location of the lighting and sound consoles is referred to as FOH, because it is generally located in the audience areas.

Gobo   A piece of metal or glass that is placed between the lamp and lens of a lighting fixture. Gobos are used to project images and shapes.

Grand Master   A fader on a console providing the ability to reduce intensity of the console's output. The grand master has priority over all other intensity functions of the con

Group   A stored array of lighting fixtures within a lighting console. The selection of groups aids in quick fixture selections during programming.

Hard Edge Light   A lighting fixture capable of focusing on an image such as a gobo or framing shutter. This type of fixture is primarily used for projection of images and shapes.

HTP   Highest takes precedence. A console function that gives priority to the highest numeric values of fixture parameters, regardless of when they are changed.

Inhibitive Master   Similar to a grand master, but only works with a defined set of fixtures.

LD   Lighting Designer.

Look *See* Cue.

LTP Latest takes precedence. A console function that gives priority to the most current changes to fixture parameters regardless of their numeric values.

MIDI Musical Instrument Device Interface.

Operator A person who is responsible for playback of cues on a lighting console.

Page A term used to describe a series of cuelists laid out in an organized fashion. Multiple pages are often used to allow for a greater number of playbacks on a console.

Palette A reference to specific values of fixture parameters. Palettes can be recorded into cues in place of actual parameter values.

Parameter A function of a lighting fixture is referred to as a parameter.

Patch The information in the console that relates the fixture numbers to the DMX addresses of the lighting fixtures and dimmers.

Playback The function of recalling stored information from a console.

Plot A diagram of the lighting fixtures and their placement. Usually also contains information regarding DMX addressing of the fixtures.

Preset *See* Cue.

Programmer The best people on Earth!

Programmer (Window) A screen or window on a lighting console that displays the currently edited information.

Rate The speed of a chase or effect.

Rig The entire lighting system, including mounting points, trussing, fixtures, and console.

Sequence An organized list of cues or steps.

Show Control External triggers used to send commands to or from a lighting console.

SMPTE Society of Motion Picture and Television Engineers is a professional body that sets and defines technical standards. Their timecode format is referenced in this book.

Timecode Timing information embedded onto audio or video tracks.

Timing Values applied to crossfades of lighting fixture parameters.

Tracking A console function where only changed values are recorded into cues. A value will remain the same until it is changed by another cue or console function.

Visualizer A software platform used with a lighting controller to graphically emulate real-world lighting situations.

Wash A lighting area or look designed to completely cover the stage or surface with color or gobos. Derived from the phrase "bathed in light."

Wash Light A lighting fixture not capable of focusing on gobos or framing shutters. This type of fixture is primarily used for broad strokes of color.

Index

Notes